Sunshine Chinese Teachers' Guidebook 1

阳光汉语教师手册

主　编　刘　骏〔美〕
(Jun Liu)

商務印書館
2011年·北京

主　　编：Jun Liu〔美〕

编　　者：王秀卿　易　文

英文审订：梅　皓

Preface

As we all know, there are two critical factors affecting the learning of a foreign language. One is the environment in which learners are exposed to the language in its cultural surroundings and they can pick up the language and use it on almost all occasions because the society functions in that language. The other is the age of learning a language, with or without the language environment. It is a common belief that the earlier learners start acquiring a foreign language, the better they will learn as a result. Many studies on younger learners' learning of foreign languages suggest that there is a "critical period." Children who start learning a foreign language before the age of 13 or 14 are able to acquire pronunciation and intonation of that language more naturally.Correct pronunciation and intonation will, in return, help learn vocabulary, ease communication, and boost self-confidence.

There are many success stories about early learning of a foreign language, such as Canadian early immersion programs and bilingual programs in many US elementary schools. But there are few examples of successful learning of Chinese as a foreign language for children, especially younger children. Apart from the lack of sufficient teachers, effective methodology and comprehensive curricula, a major reason is the lack of age-appropriate materials that are fun-filled, quick to learn, and easy to assess.

As such, we have designed and developed our Chinese for Youth series titled "Sunshine Chinese" that caters to elementary and junior high students as they develop the basic communicative competence in Chinese language. This series is the first attempt to align the vocabulary and language functions with the Youth Chinese Test (YCT) developed by Hanban (Office of Chinese Language Teaching International). This YCT-friendly textbook series will greatly assist learners with self-assessment and provide needed feedback for teachers to understand their learners' learning outcome unit after unit and book after book in the series. The theme story, which weaves through the entire series of four textbooks, is contextualized in an international school in China where children from all parts of the world are befriended in a multicultural and supportive environment. Our rationale for Sunshine Chinese is: Experience Chinese, Understand China, and Appreciate the World.

It has taken an entire team's dedication to this project for the last couple of years. As series editor, I would first and foremost thank the leadership of the Commercial Press, Duputy Director Dr. Hongbo Zhou whose insight, determination, and steady support have been impeccable. I would give my special thanks to Yueyan Liu whose continuous engagement, high responsibility, and seamless coordination have made this series possible. My sincere gratitude and appreciation also go to the entire team: Dr. Huiping Wei, Professor Xiuqing Wang, Master Teacher Wen Yi, Dr. Yuemei Wu, and Professor Yanfeng Zhao and Professor Yanlan Zhang for their expertise, experience, and great synergies in shaping and reshaping the textbooks in this series. Special thanks also goes to Hanban, esp. colleagues in the Examination Division. Their guidance, critiques, as well as suggestions have made this series more aligned to YCT. As the characters grow in the series, so do our authors' confidence, enthusiasm, and expectations.

As the Vice President of the International Society of Chinese Language Teaching (ISCLT), senior consultant of Hanban, I am excited about this first-ever YCT-friendly book series. I sincerely hope that this series will be adopted by as many schools as possible. Through the feedback and input, we, together, will make this series better as the next generation of multilingual talents develop to make this world a better place for us all.

Jun Liu

Series Editor, Sunshine Chinese

TABLE OF CONTENTS

How to Use This Book

The Teachers' Guidebook is specially designed to go with the Chinese Textbooks. It is designed to be a helpful teaching resource.

There are 4 main parts in each unit.

1. **Lesson objectives** comprise *language* and *culture*. Language objectives provides concise and specific descriptions of the skills students are expected to gain, while cultural notes are the cultural aspects tied to the language points in each unit, which feature greetings, concepts of family, holidays, history, geography and other topics of interest pertaining to Chinese culture. Various cultural notes are offered in different units according to their contents, allowing teachers to select what is needed according to their students' age, proficiency, and skills.
2. **Target Vocabulary and Sentence Structures** list the language items and sentence structures that are the foci of each lesson and on which students will be assessed.
3. **Suggested Activities** play a major part in this guidebook, with a large variety of activities including games, songs, projects for classroom and out of school settings as well.

   Based on the different phases of learning, these activities are categorized into *Guided Practice* and *Independent Practice.* In *Guided Practice*, we emphasize the role of the teacher in guiding students through these activities, and the focus is more on receptive skills in terms of comprehension and following instructor's directions. In *Independent Practice* following *Guided Practice*, we focus gradually on learners' independent skills and critical thinking, and place more emphasis on helping learners build productive skills where the teacher is more of a facilitator. In this phase, students are ready for conversations using the target language (vocabulary and/or sentence structures), and they can actually produce output (being able to express their ideas and thoughts in speaking and/or writing) in addition to input (being able to understand and interpret written and spoken language).

   Activities for *Guided Practice* are to practice listening comprehension and reading (recognizing new language items), usually used right after the new language items are taught when students can comprehend and recognize the new language items (e.g., through listening and reading), but are not ready for reproduction themselves (e.g., through speaking and writing). Activities for *Independent Practice* are designed to provide practice for integrating skills including listening, speaking, reading and writing. For the sake of convenience, reproducible materials, such as worksheets, coloring pages and cut-outs are provided in the Students' *Workbook*. These activities with the worksheets available in the *Workbook* are marked with " Workbook ".

We provide a large range of activities for each category in each unit. This allows teachers to pick and choose the activities that are best suited to the students' levels, age and needs. There are instructions for each game, which give clear explanations for how the game is to be played.

4. The last part is the **Assessment**, which is provided for each unit and covers all the new language items, including tools for assessment of listening, reading and speaking.

To avoid repetition, for frequently used games such as **Fly Swatter, Bingo, Simon Says, Dot-to-dot, Hot Potato, Teacher vs. Students,** and **Mixed -up-Sentences**, a clear explanation of each is provided at the end of this book. Please see the Appendix for instructions.

In addition, two tests are provided which match the requirement of YCT, one of which is a Mid term test (testing the first six units), and the other is a final test (testing 12 units in book one). These two tests offer a good sample for teachers and students to get familiarized with YCT in terms of its content, style and difficulty, as well as a tool for teaching and learning evaluation. "Combining teaching with exams" is the main teaching idea in the Sunshine Chinese, so it is suggested that tests be employed in the process of teaching to activate students' interest and enhance their motivation.

A MP3 is provided with rich teaching samples, for example, songs from the *Workbook*, texts reading, text slide show, and YCT-Friendly tests.

UNIT 1

我的家

LESSON OBJECTIVES

Language

Students will be able to

- Address family members in Chinese.
- Understand and use “的”（我的家，我的爸爸，我的妈妈，我的狗……）.

Culture

Students will understand

- There are different terms for big brothers/sisters and young brothers/sisters in Chinese. Traditionally, the older siblings are supposed to take more responsibility in the family, helping parents with chores, and helping take care of younger ones. Thus, the older brother/sister and younger brother/sister have different roles and responsibilities in a family and are differentiated lexically.

- Chinese family size, relationships, parents’ attitude towards their children’s education, and how they address each other.
  - Family size in China (nuclear family) is typically 3 (father, mother, and child).
  - Relationships are tight in China whereas the parents (almost always) take a very active role in raising their children in China.
  - In China, parents might be very much willing to sacrifice their own lifestyle to support their children’s education. Education is highly respected and valued in China where people believe that education determines the outcome to everything about a person and a country’s future. Therefore for their children’s education, many Chinese parents are willing to spend substantial time and energy to support their children’s future.
  - In China, parents or grandparents call their children typically by their nick names or given names, while children call their parents Dad（爸爸）and Mum（妈妈）and call their grandparents Grandpa（爷爷/姥爷）and Grandma（奶奶/ 姥姥). Another interesting aspect is the way to address in-laws. In China, most women call their husbands’ parents father and mother, while men may call their in-laws

either father and mother or uncle and aunt depending on the local tradition of where you are and the specific family dynamics.

TARGET VOCABULARY AND SENTENCE STRUCTURE

Vocabulary

我	爸爸	妈妈	姐姐	哥哥
家	狗	爱	的	

Sentence Structure

（Pronoun/Noun/Name）的（Noun） ……

（的 functions as a possessive, e.g. 我的……，爸爸的……，妈妈的……）

SUGGESTED ACTIVITIES

Guided Practice

- Use flashcards or your own family photos to introduce family members.

- Game: Fly Swatters or Bingo.

  Preparation

  Prepare a visual of the vocabulary pictures

  Game play

  -Students are divided into two teams and line up into two lines. The first person in each line (team) has a fly swatter.

  -The teacher says a word, and the person who hits the visual first wins one point for the team.

- Game

  Each student picks a flash card, and when the teacher calls out a title（爸爸，妈妈……）, the one who has that card stands up and repeats. The student who has the card without responding will be "out".

- Read and Paste **Workbook**
  Ask students to cut out the Chinese characters and glue them around the appropriate family photos.

- Family Tree **Workbook**
  Ask the students to draw their family members on the family tree. Then they can color their family tree.

- Family Story Book **Workbook**
  Ask students to draw their family members according to each Chinese sentence. Then, they write their family members' names. Cut out their real family member pages and staple them together to make a story book. Divide students into several groups and encourage them to share their Chinese family story books with each other. They can keep the mini Chinese books in the classroom.

Independent Practice

- Game: We Are Family
  Prepare three or four sets of family flash cards; each set having its own color. Ask each student to pick one. Those with the same color will form one family. Then each family with one featured color will introduce them to the rest of the class by saying "我的家，我的爸爸，我的妈妈" after practicing with their own families.

- Ask students to use their own family photos to introduce their family to the class.

- Match **Workbook**
  Ask students to match the Chinese sentences with the right person in the pictures. Then, ask them to describe the pictures in Chinese.

- Family Photo **Workbook**
  Ask students to bring a real family photo and glue it on this page. Ask them to write family member words in Chinese around the photo. The teacher collects all the family photos and later exhibits them .

- Let's Sing **Workbook**

  Teach the students to sing this song with the corresponding sign language. Ask students to teach this song to their family.

♪♫ 我爱我的家 ♪♫

这是我的家，哥哥姐姐爸爸妈妈，
我爱我的爸爸，我爱我的妈妈。
这是我的家，哥哥姐姐爸爸妈妈，
那是我的狗狗，我爱我的家。
我爱我的爸爸，我爱我的妈妈，
我爱我的姐姐，我爱我的哥哥，
我爱我的爸爸，我爱我的妈妈，
我爱我的哥哥姐姐，我爱我的家。

ASSESSMENT

Listening

Under the picture, mark 1st, 2nd, 3rd, and 4th according to the sequence the teacher calls them.

Reading

Match the words with proper pictures.

wǒ de māma 1. 我 的 妈妈	E	wǒ de jiějie 2. 我 的 姐姐	
wǒ de bàba 3. 我 的 爸爸		wǒ de gǒu 4. 我 的 狗	
wǒ de gēge 5. 我 的 哥哥		wǒ de jiā 6. 我 的 家	

A

B

C

D

E

F

Speaking

1. Introduce the family members on your family photos.
2. Tell the family story “我的家”.

UNIT 2

你好

LESSON OBJECTIVES

Language

Students will be able to

- Greet and part in Chinese by using phrases “你好” and “再见”.
- Introduce themselves in Chinese by saying “我叫……”.
- Ask people’s names: “你叫什么？”

Culture

Students will understand

- Where is China?
  Use a World map to show the location of China in the world.
- What is the word order in a Chinese name?
  In Chinese names, the family name always comes first as a sign of respect for family ancestors, followed by the given name.
- Do Chinese people hug or kiss for greetings and saying goodbye?
  Chinese people do not hug or kiss even between families. A handshake is common on some formal occasions for greetings or saying goodbye in modern times, but when someone from a culture that hugs as a greeting greets a Chinese, the Chinese person is usually happy to reciprocate.
- How many people are studying Chinese language in the world? And how many international students are studying Chinese in China? (http://www.hanban.edu.cn)
- Chinese *Kung Fu*
  Anyone who has seen classical Chinese Kung Fu movies a good impression of Chinese Kung Fu or Chinese martial arts. In the west, Bruce Lee, Jackie Chan, and Jet Li are among the most famous Chinese film stars adept in *Kung Fu*. Ask students whether they know of them and what and how much they know about them. Use a powerpoint presentation or some pictures of these famous movie stars to help the discussion. Two points should be emphasized One is *Kung Fu* martial art, and its sister sport *Tai Chi Chuan* 太极拳, is a sporting exercise that focuses on mental discipline, as well as an artistic form. It is used to maintain fitness, cure

illness, enhance longevity, and for self-defense. It is also a comprehensive template for culturing the human body. Another point a teacher might want to mention to the students is that not all Chinese people practice *Kung Fu* or *Tai Chi Chuan*.
More related information on: http://kungfu.chinese.cn/

TARGET VOCABULARY AND SENTENCE STRUCTURE

Vocabulary

好　叫　什么　你好　再见　谢谢

Structures

1. (Pronoun/Noun)叫什么?
2. (Pronoun/Noun)叫……
3. 你好!
4. 再见!
5. 谢谢。

SUGGESTED ACTIVITIES

Guided Practice

- Presentation on China using a powerpoint with some simple facts about China: capital, provinces (instead of states like in US), biggest city, 3rd largest country in the world in terms of landmass, 1st in population, language (Mandarin Chinese with a number of other dialects), the Great Wall, Pandas, the national flag, Chinese map (said to look like a rooster).

- Match Workbook
  After introducing how to greet each other in Chinese, you can help students play the matching game. Ask the students to match Chinese greetings with the right pictures.

- Panda Fan Workbook
  Introduce more information about pandas from China and ask students to color the pandas and bamboo with the right colors. Cut out the big fan and make the paper fan with small sticks. The students can then take the panda fans home or hang them up in the classroom.

- Say “你好” to your students as you shake hands with each of them, and prompt them to respond.

Independent Practice

- Gather students in a circle and play a name game. Clap and chant in a singsong style, “你好，你好，我叫……” . Encourage students to clap along with you.
  - Gesture to the student to your left (or right) and say, “你好，你好，你叫什么？” , prompt the student to respond.
  - Shake the student's hand while saying “你好，(name)!” Prompt the student to respond.

- Ask your students to greet each other by using the correct sentence structure.

- Mini Play
  Ask one volunteer to the front of the classroom, and greet him/her by saying “你好” , he/she should say “你好” back. Then, turn around and wave, and saying “再见” and prompting him/her to respond. Invite more students up to do this with you. When you are sure they know what “再见” means and can say it correctly, put your students into pairs and repeat the same conversation. Have the students switch partners and repeat the game.

- Before the class, stand at the door and greet each student by saying “你好” . And ask the students to do the same to their classmates. Say “再见” when the class is over.

- Prepare two big flashcards of “你好” and “再见” , ask kids to pick one. After a student picks one, he/she says what is on the card. If he/she is correct, he/she goes to pick another student and continue the game.

- Give your students Chinese names, assist them in making name tags, and ask students to decorate their name tags. In the lessons to follow, they can use them in various activities.

- My Portrait **Workbook**
  Ask students to draw themselves on sheets of paper and try to write their Chinese names with your help. Ask them to glue their portraits to their Chinese books or folders.

- Story Book **Workbook**
  Tell students the chanted story about panda using body language. Ask students to color the story book and chant along together.

- Let's Sing **Workbook**
  Teacher teaches the students to sing this song with the sign language. Ask students to teach this song to their family.

♪♫ 你好 ♪♫

你好！你好！
我很好，我很好。
我和你，你和我。
真快乐，真快乐。

ASSESSMENT

Listening

Teacher will say “你好”“再见”“谢谢”. Please judge the pictures with “√” or “×” according to the sentences you hear.

1. 		3. 	
2. 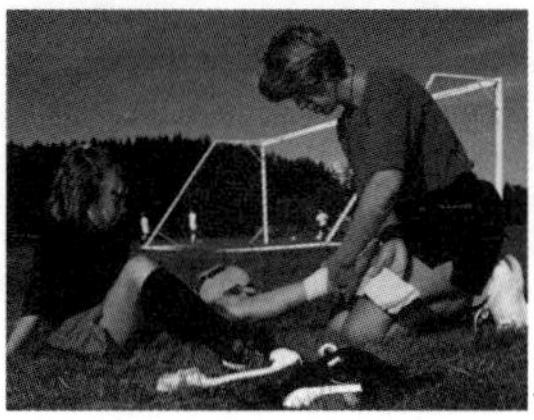			

Reading

Match the words or sentences with proper pictures.

Nǐ hǎo! Wǒ jiào Tom. Nǐ hǎo! Wǒ jiào Mike. 1. A: 你好！我 叫 Tom。 B: 你好！ 我 叫 Mike。	
Zàijiàn! 2. A: 再见！	
Tā zài nàr. Xièxie! 3. A: 他 在 那儿。 B: 谢谢！	

A

B

C

Speaking

1. Work in pairs, greeting each other in Chinese.
2. Introduce yourself to the teacher.

UNIT 3 你几岁

LESSON OBJECTIVES

Language

Students will be able to

- Count and write numbers from one to ten in Chinese.
- Ask and answer questions about age : 你几岁？ 我……岁。
- Offer congratulations on the event of a birthday: 生日快乐！
- Express gratitude: 谢谢！
- Write from “一” to “十”.

Culture

Students will grasp

- Basic knowledge of Chinese writing

  1. Chinese is a non-alphabetic language while English is a language that employs an alphabet for its writing system. Therefore, words in Chinese are written in Chinese characters formed with strokes while words in English are formed with various combinations of the 26 letters.

  2. The five basic strokes for Chinese characters writing are “— 丨 丿 ㇏ 丶”.

  3. The order in which strokes are written (commonly referred to as “stroke order”) is generally from left to right; top to bottom; with horizontal lines drawn first, and vertical lines later; for box-like characters like “四”, the rule is to “fill the container before you close it”.

- Lucky and unlucky numbers in China and the logic behind

  The lucky numbers and unlucky numbers in China mainly depend on their pronunciation. The number “8” has a similar pronunciation to the word “fa” （发）, meaning becoming wealthy. There is a good deal of attention paid to this by businessmen, and they are known to choose the 8th of the month as their company’s opening date. Additionally, they prefer to spend extra money to buy phone numbers or license plates ending with the number “8”. The opening ceremony of Beijing Olympic Games was arranged to commence at 8:00 pm,

August 8, in 2008. Six "liu" sounds like "溜" in Chinese, the latter of the two having the meaning of "to go smoothly". Nine sounds like "jiu"（久）, a word that connotes durability or "lasting long". Today, many Chinese like to arrange weddings to fall on a date that includes a nine, in the hope that their marriage will last forever.

Four, in Chinese, sounds like "死" meaning death, and it is the unluckiest number, which is disliked by most Chinese people. Many people try to avoid having this number used in their phone numbers or license plates if at all possible. The number "250" is a joke number that is used to refer to someone as a fool.

With regards to lucky and unlucky numbers in Western (or local) culture, you may ask your students and let them be your teacher!

TEACHING TIP

Show students the phone numbers or vehicle license plate numbers of yours and your Chinese friends, or wedding days or some other important days for Chinese people to give them a taste of the Chinese number culture.

- How do Chinese people celebrate birthdays?

  Chinese people normally celebrate their birthdays by having a dinner party with a birthday cake and candles. The birthday person receives gifts from his/her parents, family, and friends. Besides a lot of good dishes, in particular noodles are served on birthdays as they bring good wishes of longevity for the birthday person: noodles are long.

  There are several special birthdays in a person's life in China. "The One Hundredth Day", "One Year Old", 60th and 66th birthday, are special birthdays for Chinese people. The teacher may mention the special celebration of One Year Old birthday: a selection of objects on a table or cloth is put before the child. He/she will be asked to pick one. The choice that the child makes is believed to be an indication of what the child will become one day.

  For more information about Chinese birthday celebration, please refer to: http://www.helium.com/items/721639-guide-to-chinese-birthday-customs

  The following link offers more information about how to choose gifts to Chinese people: http://www.cp.com.cn:8245/cf/newsdetail.cfm?iCntno=1007&iPage=2

TEACHING TIP

Have a birthday party with your students in Chinese fashion. Your students will know more about the birthday celebration in China by experiencing it themselves.

TARGET VOCABULARY AND SENTENCE STRUCTURE

Vocabulary

一　二　三　四　五　六　七　八　九　十　几　岁　生日　快乐

Sentence Structures

1. (Pronoun/Noun)几岁？
2. (Pronoun/Noun)(number)岁。

SUGGESTED ACTIVITIES

Guided Practice

- Bingo
- Fly Swatter
- Teacher Versus Students
- Dot – to – Dot
- Match Workbook
  Match the Chinese characters with finger pictures.
- Friendship Circle

Ask the whole class to stand like a big friendship circle and take turns to count numbers from 1-10. If a given student's number is 5 or 10, he/she has to sit down. The one who stands last will be the winner.

- Monkey King Workbook
  On the body of the Monkey King, there are some numbers written in Chinese characters. Follow the color key with these numbers to color the Monkey King correctly. This is to practice reading Chinese numbers characters.

Independent Practice

- Rope Skipping
  Prepare a rope and ask volunteers to skip the rope. While a student is skipping, the rest of the class will count together in Chinese. Make sure that you jot down on your note how many reps each participant skips, and reward the one who skips the most.

- Math in Chinese Class
  Ask students to do maths like "1+2" = ? or "9 - ( ) =5". Kids will love it!

- Let's Keep in Touch
  Making a Phone Book. Students take turns to tell his/her home phone number or cell phone number in Chinese, and the rest of the class is to write it down in his/her notebook. You may tell your students your phone number in China, and then you will tell them how to call China from the country you are in (you need to dial the country code, area code, and the phone number). Share with them the time difference between China and the country you are in.

- Finger Counting
  Show students how to use the five fingers of one hand to show ten numbers, then you or some students do the hand language, the rest say it out. Please note that the sign language used by Chinese may be different from that in other countries. Should this happen to be the case, please use comparison and contrast strategies to highlight the symbolic meanings contained in Chinese handcounting.

- Who Picks up Most
  Take some chopsticks and marbles to your class, divide students into groups, practice picking up marbles using chopsticks, then stage a competition to see which group picks up most.
  Each person from each group is given one minute; when time is up, the second

person continues till every one of the group has had his/her turn. One scorekeeper should be chosen and write the scores of each group on the board. Reward the winning group. When one person is doing the picking, the rest of the class is supposed to count the marbles he/she picks in Chinese.

> **TEACHING TIP**
> Note: when students are practicing using chopsticks to pick up marbles, you may need to walk around to provide some necessary help.

- Dance
  Make your own dance based on the Chinese Sixteen Steps.
  While you are leading the dance, ask your students to count the steps together with you in Chinese. Later when your students are familiar enough with the concept, you may dance to the music.

- Count and Write Numbers **Workbook**
  Count and write down the numbers in Chinese.

- Let's Sing **Workbook**
  Encourage students to sing the Chinese song with the corresponding handshapes.

♪♫ 一二三 ♪♫

一、二、三，三、二、一，

一、二、三、四、五、六、七，

七、六、五、四、三、二、一。

- Let's Chant **Workbook**
  Encourage students sing the Chinese chant with handshapes.

♪♫ 一二三四五 ♪♫

一、二、三、四、五，

姐姐妹妹来跳舞，

六、七、八、九、十，

哥哥弟弟来吟诗。

- Let’s Sing Workbook

♪♫ 一二三四五六七 ♪♫
一二三四五六七，
我的朋友在哪里？
在中国，
在美国，
我的朋友在这里。

- Let’s Sing Workbook

♪♫ 祝你生日快乐 ♪♫
祝你生日快乐，
祝你生日快乐。
祝你生日快乐，
祝你生日快乐。

- Draw the Candles Workbook
  Ask the students to read the four conversations depicted in the pictures, then draw the candles on the blank birthday cake and decorate the cake with crayons.

- Use the Chinese Brush Pen
  Give students the paper with 田字格(traditional paper with the shape of 田 for each character with the ease to practice strokes) and Chinese brush pen. Show them how to hold the brush and the right pose while writing calligraphy. You might give your students a brief introduction of the appreciation of Chinese calligraphy and basic rules, styles, and skills in practicing calligraphy.

ASSESSMENT

Listening

Listen to the sentences and if they are right, write "✓", if they are wrong, write " × ".

1.		
2.		
3.		
4.		
5.		

Reading

Write the Chinese Character according to the pictures.

 四	

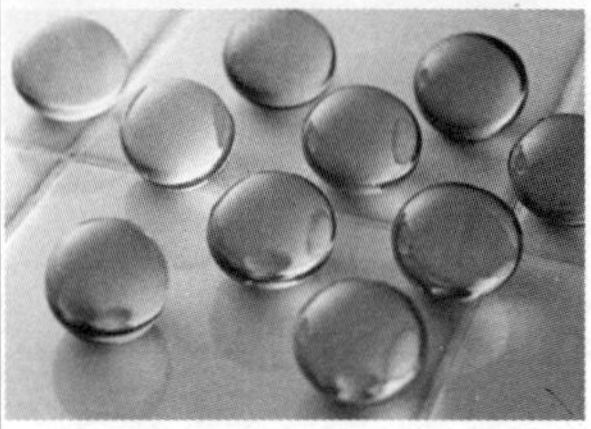	

Speaking

1. Ask students to read some phone numbers you gave them on notecards.
2. Dialogue with a partner:你几岁？我____岁。

UNIT 4

我喜欢

LESSON OBJECTIVES

Language

Students will be able to

- Identify and name body parts
- Express liking something by using "喜欢"

Culture

- Monkey King and Zhu Bajie
  Monkey King and Zhu Bajie are two main characters in a famous book, *Journey to the West* in China. Use a slideshow or pictures to help you with your explanation. Tell students briefly about the story or take them to the computer lab so that they may search for this interesting story. Make a project called "*Journey to the West*". You can hang the posters on a wall of the classroom or in the hallway.

- What do Chinese people look like?
  Ask your students to tell the difference in appearance between you and them in terms of hair color, size of nose, eye color, etc.. This can be done at the very beginning of the lesson as a warm-up activity or in the very end as a way to practice the language points and as a cultural awareness activity to enhance their cultural sensitivities.

TARGET VOCABULARY AND SENTENCE STRUCTURE

Vocabulary

喜欢　手　头发　眼睛　鼻子　头　耳朵　他　她

Sentence Structure

(Pronoun/Noun)喜欢 (Pronoun/Noun)

SUGGESTED ACTIVITIES

Guided Practice:

- Bingo
- Fly Swatters
- Teacher VS Students
- Simon Says
- Match **Workbook**
  Ask the students to match the pictures with corresponding Chinese sentences.
- My Robot **Workbook**
  Tell students to imagine they can create a robot for themselves. First, they have to pick one or more traits provided in Chinese for the robot, then draw the other body parts to finish the robot drawing. Glue the Chinese words on the line to finish the sentence starting with "我喜欢".
- Story Book **Workbook**
  Students read the Chinese sentences with teacher's help, draw the body parts for each page, then staple them to make story book and share their stories. Then sing the song in Chinese.

Independent Practice

- Divide students into pairs and play Simon Says, with each student taking turns to be Simon.
- Game: Follow the Leader

Lead students around the room and call out "Shake your 头", "Touch your 鼻子" "Raise your 手". Prompt students to follow your promptings. (This activity, can also be used as a guided practice). As the game continues, leave out body parts and prompt students to fill in the blanks. For example, shake your hands and only say, "Shake your ____." Prompt students to say, "手" to complete your sentence and shake their hands. Rotate students into the lead. Continue the game, practicing all the target language about body parts.
(After the students become good at this game, the teacher can speak only Chinese for the directions: 摇摇头，摸摸鼻子，举举手)

- Monkey King and Zhu Bajie **Workbook**
  Color them, talk with each other about their body parts (eyes, ears, nose, hands, head) by saying "他的……, 我喜欢他的……".

- Trace Me
  Instruction: Divide students into different groups, trace one person on a big piece of paper, then glue the words of different body parts on the right place on the paper. (This is to practice recognizing the words)

- Debate: Who is Most Important
  Instruction: Designate 6 students as 手，头发，耳朵，眼睛，鼻子，and头 respectively, each holds up his/her own flashcard of the body part word, and debate which part of the body is the most important. They can use English for the debate but they have to speak Chinese for the body part.

- Let's Sing **Workbook**

♪♫ 我喜欢 ♪♫

我喜欢他的头，他的头，
我喜欢他的手，他的手，
我喜欢他的眼睛，他的眼睛，
你好，你好，再见，再见。
我喜欢他的耳朵，他的耳朵，
我喜欢她的鼻子，她的鼻子，
我喜欢她的头发，她的头发。
你好，你好，再见，再见。

ASSESSMENT

Listening

The teacher says the words for the body parts in Chinese, and students are to mark 1st, 2nd, 3rd, 4th, 5th and 6th on the picture according to what they hear from the teacher.

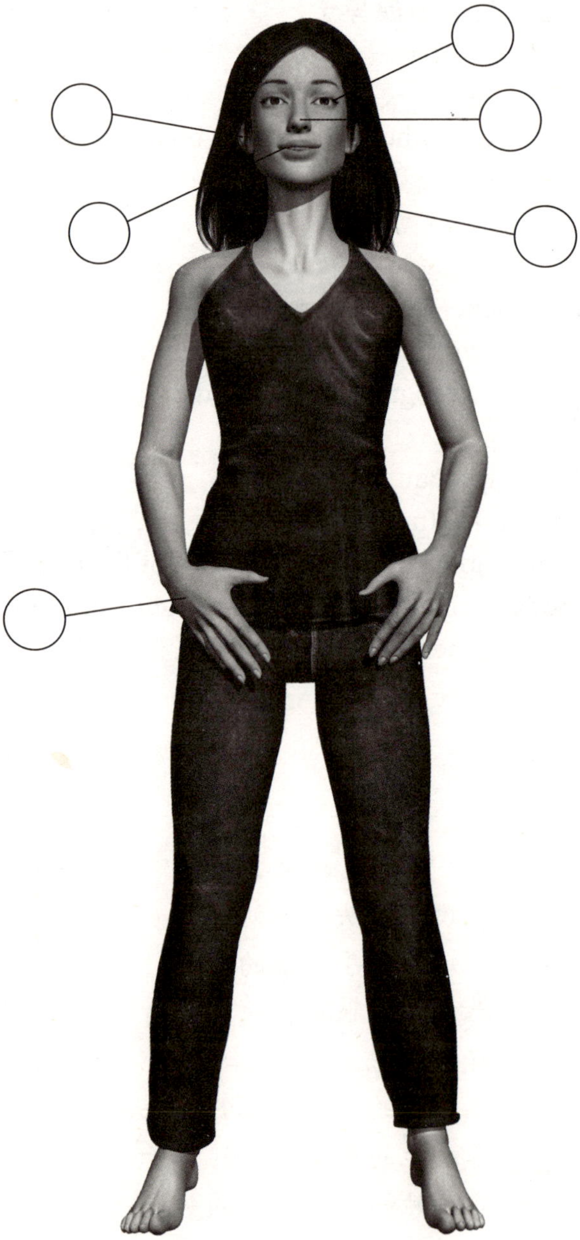

Reading

1. Draw your hero: Draw your own hero, and write the words for each different body part on the right places on the hero's body.

2. The activities "**Match**", "**My Robot**", and "**Story Book**" in the **Workbook** can be used as the assessment activities.

Speaking

1. Students work in pairs: one names the 6 body parts learned in this unit, one points to the corresponding points on his/her own body.
2. Point to oneself and say: 我的头，我的眼睛……, 我喜欢我的眼睛/手…….
3. Draw your favorite cartoon person, introduce him/her to the class by saying: 我喜欢她/他的……（头，头发，眼睛，耳朵，嘴，鼻子，手）.

UNIT 5

你去哪儿

LESSON OBJECTIVES

Language

Students will be able to

- Talk about where one is going.
- Understand and use the words about places: "商店、学校".

Culture

- Students will be able to understand that "你去哪儿" can be a greeting between acquaintances in China, but not between people who meet for the first time. It would be a very natural and friendly conversation if you ask your Chinese friends where they are going when you meet each other on the road. To Chinese people, it's a good way to show your close relationship. However, it's not a suitable question to ask amongst people meeting each other for the first time.

- A brief introduction of international students going to schools in China.
  Nowadays, more and more foreigners come to China with their family members. Their kids are immersed in China, acquiring the Chinese language and are exposed to Chinese culture. In most cities in China, there are many schools that accept international students. There are many international schools, too. It's very interesting and rewarding for students to study in China with classmates from different countries of different cultures.

  For more information on the international schools in China, please check the following links for two international schools in Beijing and Shanghai: http://www.biss.com.cn/; http://www.fis.net.cn/

TARGET VOCABULARY AND SENTENCE STRUCTURE

Vocabulary

去　哪儿　商店　学校　我们

Sentence Structures

1. (Pronoun/Noun)去哪儿?
2. (Pronoun/Noun)去(place)

SUGGESTED ACTIVITIES

Guided Practice

- Fly Swatters Game
  There should be both Chinese characters and pictures of these places on the cards. You should paste these cards on the board.

去	哪儿	商店	商店	学校	你们	我们

- Put three big flashcards with 商店，学校，Linda 家 in three corners of the classroom. Order your students to go to different places, and your students will go according to your instruction. For example, you say, "Mary，你去学校", and Mary will understand you and go to the corner with "学校" flashcard. With the game continuing, the teacher can ask two or more students at the same time, saying "Mary，Linda，Chelsea，你们去……".

- Find the Places Workbook
  Students choose the Chinese words matching a specific place, and Paste these words onto the right pictures in the work sheet.

Independent Practice

- Chain-practice

  Put three big flashcards with "商店，学校，Linda 家" in three corners of the classroom. Line the students in one line. The teacher can be the first in the line and say loudly to the student behind him/her, "我去学校（商店/Linda 家），你去哪儿", prompt that student to answer and ask the student behind him/her, "我去商店（Linda 家），你去哪儿". They will go to where they say. When the game is done, students will be in three places of the classroom.

- The Most Popular Places

  - Make place cards of "学校，商店，家". Paste these cards in different corners of the classroom.

  - Choose one volunteer to stand beside each card. If someone comes to his/her card, he/she should say: "你好".

  - Let other students stand in line, as the teacher asks a question to each of them in turn.

  Teacher: (Students' name in Chinese), 你去哪儿?

  Student: 我去学校（商店/……家）。

  - Students go to the places they said and stand beside the cards after greeting with the volunteers there.

  - After all students have chosen proper cards, each volunteer should count how many people stand beside his/her card. Then the most popular place will be selected.

- Draw the Places **Workbook**

  Students read the conversation and draw the place they will go in the bubble. Then, the teacher should encourage them to practice the conversations.

- Role-playing Game

  Group your students first. Each team has 5 members. They will take the roles of mom, dad, Tom, Lily, and Bobi. Then they will practice the dialogue according to the text. If there are less than 5 students in your class, you may assign two roles to one person.

- Hot Potato Game (for practicing the target sentence structure)

- Let's Write **Workbook**

  Trace the character "家", color it and write it. Give your student a paper with the character with its stroke order shown.

- Read and Paste **Workbook**
  Read the Chinese sentences and the pictures, guess where they are going, paste the Chinese sentences in the corresponding bubbles.

- Let's Chant **Workbook**
  Sing and color.

♪♫ 你去哪儿 ♪♫

你好，你好，你去哪儿？
爸爸，妈妈，你们去哪儿？
我们去商店，我们去商店。
哥哥，姐姐，你们去哪儿？
我们去学校，我们去学校。
Bobbi，Bobbi，你去哪儿？
我去Linda家，我去Linda家。

- Let's Sing **Workbook**
  Sing and color.

♪♫ 你们去哪儿 ♪♫

你好，你好，爸爸妈妈，你们去哪儿？
我们去呀去商店，我们去呀，去呀，去商店。
你好，你好，哥哥姐姐，你们去哪儿？
我们去呀去学校，我们去呀，去呀，去呀，去学校。

ASSESSMENT

Listening

The teacher will say 4 sentences. Please judge the pictures according to the sentences you hear.

1. 	2. 
3. 	4. 

Reading

Match the sentences with the proper pictures.

Māma qù shāngdiàn. 1. 妈妈 去 商店。		Tā qù Linda jiā. 2. 她 去 Linda 家。	
Gēge zài gōngyuán. 3. 哥哥 在 公园。		Wǒmen zài xuéxiào. 4. 我们 在 学校。	

A

B

C

D

Speaking

Speak the sentences on the cards that you have chosen.

People		Place	
爸爸	Tracy	商店	Tom家
妈妈	贝贝	学校	我的学校
姐姐	心爱	我家	Linda家

Q: 爸爸去哪儿?
A: 爸爸去学校。

UNIT 6

这是什么

LESSON OBJECTIVES

Language

Students will be able to

- Talk about food and drink.
- Understand and use Demonstrative Pronouns（这/那）.

Culture

Students will know about

- Chinese Food

  Famous for its abundant and exquisite varieties and styles, Chinese food has taken an important part in the nation's traditional cultures. China has a long history and a vast geographic territory. Due to the diversity of the climate, products, and customs, there are widely varying food styles and tastes in local regions. Through the definition of past dynasties, the long standing cooking arts has formed rich and colorful local dishes, categorized into "the eight major cuisines": Shandong, Zhejiang, Sichuan, Jiangsu, Guangdong, Hunan, Fujian and Anhui. Chinese restaurants can be found everywhere throughout the world. Many people in various countries regard having a genuine and authentic Chinese meal as a big treat.

TEACHING TIP

The teacher may use a slideshow to demonstrate these "eight major cuisines". Please refer to the following websites for more information about Chinese food: http://college.chinese.cn/article/2009-08/25/content_12620.htm; http://www.chinatraveldepot.com/C176-Food-and-Drink-Tips

- How to use chopsticks

  Step 1: Hold one chopstick still in your thumb joint;

  Step 2: Balance the other chopstick between your index finger and middle finger;

  Step 3: Use your thumb first and then your index finger to manipulate the top chopstick in a pincer movement.

How to Use Chopsticks

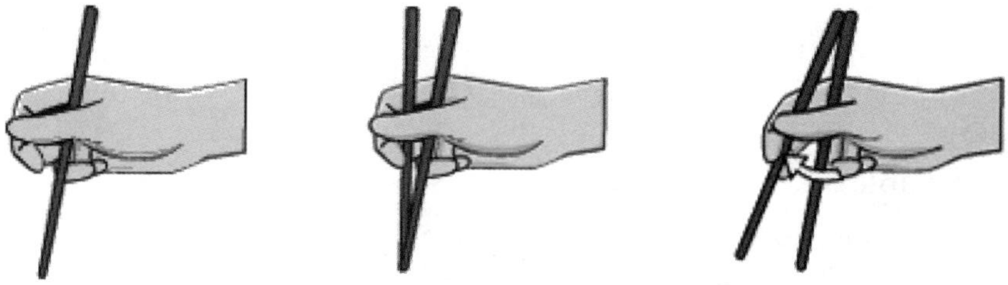

1 2 3

For more information, please refer to the link http://www.soxc.com.cn/i/en/?news-news-read-48.html

TARGET VOCABULARY AND SENTENCE STRUCTURE

Vocabulary

这 那 是 面条 米饭 苹果 可乐 什么

Sentence Structures

这是 (Pronoun/Noun)

那是 (Pronoun/Noun)

这是/那是什么？

SUGGESTED ACTIVITIES

Guided Activities

- Fly Swatters
  There should be both Chinese characters and pictures of these places on the cards, and paste the cards on the board.

- Bingo

- Teacher Versus Students

- Dot – to – Dot

- Match
  Match the food with the Chinese characters with Pinyin.

- Listen and Draw Workbook
  Ask the students to draw the food according to what they hear from their teacher.

- In the *Workbook*, there are some pictures of food: rice, noodles, apple, and a bottle of coke. The teacher says what he/she eats/drinks (我eat米饭/我drink可乐), students circle on the book accordingly.

- Be a waiter or waitress
  Take to the classroom some paper plates and cups together with some notecards for rice, noodles, apple, and coke (or you can use actual objects, but in that case be ready for some mess), put these cards into plates or cups accordingly. Call out what to eat or drink (我eat米饭/我drink可乐), and one student is chosen to take what you ordered to you. Encourage as many students as possible to participate.

- Match Workbook
  This is practice for "这是" and "那是".

- Read and Paste Workbook
  Cut out the Chinese characters and paste them to pictures of the right food.

- Draw the Food Workbook
  Draw the food as described in the Chinese sentences.

Independent Activities

- Guess what I am eating
  Ask for a volunteer to act out eating different food (rice, noodles, an apple) or drinking (coke) in front of the class. Other students guess what he/she is eating or drinking, and say it aloud.
  Pair up the students in class and repeat the game in pairs.

- Hot Potato Game
  Please see the notes at the back of this book for the instructions for the game. The flash cards for this game in this unit should be "米饭，面条，可乐，苹果". Encourage students to use "这是……" by showing the cards.

- Play the game "Be a waiter/waitress" mentioned in Guided Practice, but ask a student to give orders. Students take turns to make the order.

- Guess what it is
  Two students do this game together in front of the class. One chooses a flash card of either food or drink and paste (or stick) it on the back of the other student, and make him/her guess what the flash card is by saying: "那是什么?" He/she should make the guess by saying "那是……". The guesser can take up to 3 tries. After 3 tries if he/she still can not guess right, he/she is out of the game.

- Get the ball and answer my question
  The teacher throws a soft ball to a student. After the student gets the ball, the teacher picks up a flashcard and points to the picture on the card asking "这是什么". Prompt students to use the sentence structure "那是……". A student who fails to understand or answer is out of the game.

- Guess what's in my hand
  Prepare flashcards of the food or drink learned in this unit (rice, noodles, apples, and coke). Ask one student (say student A) to go outside of the classroom, and let another student (say student B) to choose one flashcard and put it in his hand. Student A comes in the room and Student B greets him/her and waves his/her fist asking "这是什么". There are at most three tries. After 3 incorrect guesses a student is out.

- Do a Survey Workbook
  Survey 1: Ask students to make a survey about what food and drinks their classmates like and dislike, in the following manner: Draw a chart on a piece of paper with students' names on the left, food and drink on the top of the chart. Address all students in the class by asking "你喜欢什么". Use a smiling face or sad face to indicate likes and dislikes. Then present their survey to the class by saying, "(name) 喜欢 (food or drink)" Or use the work sheet on the *Workbook*.

  Survey 2:
  Do the survey about the food at home. Have students ask the family their likes and dislikes about the food and drinks on the chart, draw a smiling face or sad face to indicate approval or disapproval, and share the survey in the class.

- Mini-game: Eating at a restaurant.
  Arrange students into groups. Each group chooses one student as a waiter or waitress, and the rest pretend to go to eat at the restaurant where that waiter or waitress works. They can pretend to be a family with a father, mother, brother and sister, or they can be a group of friends. They should work together to create the menu by drawing the food and drink, marking the price of each item. The "diners" can ask the waiter or waitress about the food saying, "这是什么/那是什么？" Make the order by saying "我喜欢……" or just saying the name of the food or drink. The teacher should help students understand the table manners in China, such as the absence of tipping culture, and the sharing of food among guests.

- Family Story Book Project
  Ask students to draw family members and the food and drinks each likes. Each member of the family has one page in the book. Under the food and drink, they can glue Chinese characters the teacher has written or printed for them. They can take this lovely book back home and share it with their family.

- Whispers
  Step 1: Group the students in teams and ask each team to stand in one straight line.
  Step 2: The teacher whispers to the first student of each line:
  这是苹果。
  这是面条。
  那是米饭。
  Step 3: Students whisper the sentence to the student behind.
  Step 4: The last student in each line speaks aloud the sentence.

The team that gets the exact sentence in the end wins this game.

- Act Out the Text
  Put three students in each group to act out the text. After practicing, have groups act in turn and choose the best team.

- Let's Sing Workbook

♪♫ 这是什么 ♪♫
这是什么？这是什么？这是米饭。
那是什么？那是什么？那是面条。
这是什么？这是什么？这是可乐。
那是什么？那是什么？那是苹果。

ASSESSMENT

Listening
Games "Draw the food" on Guided Practice can be used for this assessment.

Reading
Match the sentences with proper pictures.

Zhè shì mǐfàn. 1. 这是米饭。		Nà shì miàntiáo. 2. 那是面条。	
Zhè shì píngguǒ. 3. 这是苹果。		Nà shì kělè. 4. 那是可乐。	

A

B

C

D

Speaking

Describe the picture.

UNIT 7

我爱吃面条

LESSON OBJECTIVES

Language

Students should be able to talk about likes and dislikes of certain food items and drinks（爱吃……；不爱吃……；爱喝……；不爱喝……）.

Culture

Students will understand

- Eating at a restaurant in China.
  Like other countries, Chinese people eat at restaurants with their family, friends or colleagues for different reasons such as family gatherings, entertaining friends, business meals, or other social occasions. In order to attract customers, restaurant owners in China tend to decorate their restaurants in a very fancy and elaborate manner. There is usually a main hall as well as some separate private rooms. In a restaurant people can choose private rooms for privacy or comfort, which is considered desirable, but those rooms come with minimum consumption levels or a bit higher cost for food. Giving tips is not customary at restaurants in China; you pay your meal according to the cost on the bill, and no more than that.
  For the table manner and rules, please check: http://cul.chinese.cn/article/2010-06/17/content_144619.htm

  Please refer to the link http://china.citw2008.com/html/2006/1028/638.shtml for some information about the hotpot situation in China.

- Different flavors in different places in China.
  Chinese people's diets are rich, colorful, and very flavorful. Due to the country's large size, Chinese food exhibits a large variety in its flavors due to the tastes of the people in different regions. Various local cuisines have their own characteristics blended with that of their regions. Generally speaking, the food Sichuan and Hunan is known for its spicy and hot flavor and is a perennial favorite throughout China.

Popular dishes include Hot and Spicy Lobster, Poached Fish (Literally called Water Boiled Fish), and Sautéed Crab in Hot Spicy Sauce, among others. Beijing is famed for its roast meat like roast duck; food in Guangdong and Shanghai is known for its sweet flavor, and the food in the North of China is famed for being salty.

More information on the variety of Chinese food at: http://china.citw2008.com/CultureFood/Food.aspx

TARGET VOCABULARY AND SENTENCE STRUCTURE

Vocabulary

吃　喝　不　牛奶　和　水

Sentence Structures

(Pronoun/Noun)（不）爱吃/喝 (food/fruit/drink)

SUGGESTED ACTIVITIES

Guided Practice

TEACHING TIP

The food-related words learned in the previous unit can be reviewed by putting them in the following games

- Bingo
- Fly Swatters

- Draw What You Hear
  The teacher should give instructions about what he/she likes eating by saying "我爱吃面条". The students are supposed to draw noodles and a smiling face; When the teacher says "我不爱吃米饭", students will draw rice with a sad face. Give instruction about drink too as the game goes on（我不/爱喝牛奶/可乐……）.

- Match Workbook

- What does the teacher like?
  On the handouts, there are some pictures of dishes of rice, noodles, apples, a bottle of coke, and glasses of milk, the teacher says what he/she eats/drinks, and students circleitems on the paper accordingly.

- Be a waiter or waitress.
  Take to the classroom some paper plates and cups together with some notecards for rice, noodles, apples, coke, and milk (or you can use the real items, but be ready for some mess), put these cards into plates or cups accordingly. Call out what you like to eat or drink（我爱吃…… or 我爱喝……）, and one student will be chosen to take what you ordered to you. Encourage as many students to participate as possible.

- Choose the Correct Verbs Workbook
  There are pictures of some food: hamburger, rice, jiaozi, coke, water, milk, juice, etc. Give students stickers with "吃" or "喝" on them, paste them under the right food picture.

Independent Practice

- Hot Potato Game
  The flash cards for this game in this unit should be "米饭，面条，苹果，可乐，牛奶". As the game goes on, the teacher can encourage students to make sentences like "我爱吃米饭" or "我爱喝牛奶" or "我不爱吃/喝……".

- Guess what you eat and drink.
  Two students do this game together in front of the class. One chooses a flash card of either food or drink and sticks it on the back of the other student, and makes him/her guess what the flash card is by saying "你爱吃什么". He/she should make the guess as to what the food may be first by saying "我爱吃米饭/我爱吃面条". He/she is only given 3 guesses. If after 3 guesses he/she is not successful, he/she is out of the game. As the game goes on, two cards can be chosen at the same

time, prompt the student to guess “我爱吃……和……”.
Do the same game to practice drinks.

- Do the game “Be a waiter/waitress” mentioned in Guided Practice, but ask a student to give orders. Students take turns to make the order.

- Get the ball and answer my question.
The teacher throws a soft ball to a student who should answer the teacher's question “你爱吃/喝什么”. A student who fails to understand or answer is out of the game.

- Survey
Make a survey about what food and drinks your classmates like and dislike. Students should draw a chart on a piece of paper with students' name on the left, food and drinks on the top of the chart. Talk to all the kids in the class by asking “你爱吃/喝什么”. Use a smiling face or frowning face to indicate likes and dislikes or write the character “爱” depending on your students' level. Then present the survey to the class by saying “……（name）爱吃/喝……, 不爱吃/喝……”.

- Mini Play: Eating at a school cafeteria.
Divide students into groups with four students in each. Use the transcripts in the text as a model allowing them to make changes if desired. After practicing, encourage them to take turns to perform for the class.

- Family Story Book Project
Ask students to draw their family members and the food and drinks each likes and dislikes. Each member of the family has one page. Under the food and drink they like, the students are encouraged to write “爱”; and under the food and drinks they do not like, encourage students to write “不爱”. Again, this depends on the students' level. If they are not ready for writing these characters, the teacher can either let them draw a smiling face or frowning face instead or glue these characters which have been printed for them. They can take this lovely book back home and share it with their family.

- Draw the Apples **Workbook**
Draw the fruit according to the Chinese names and color them (half in red and half in green).
- Read and Paste **Workbook**

- Order foods **Workbook**

- Let's Sing **Workbook**

♪♫ 我爱喝可乐 ♪♫

我爱吃面条，我不爱吃米饭。
我爱，我爱，喝牛奶，我不爱喝水。
你呢？你呢？你爱喝什么？
我爱，我爱，我爱喝可乐。

ASSESSMENT

Listening

The teacher can order food and drinks, asking one student at a time to pretend to be the waiter to take the order.

Reading

Match the pictures with the words or sentences.

píngguǒ 1. 苹果		Tā ài hē niúnǎi. 2. 她 爱 喝 牛奶。	
niúnǎi 3. 牛奶		Tā ài chī píngguǒ. 4. 她 爱 吃 苹果。	
mǐfàn 5. 米饭		Tāmen bú ài chī miàntiáo. 6. 他们 不 爱 吃 面条。	

A

B

C

D

E

F

Speaking

1. Students make presentation about what their family members like or dislike in terms of food and drink.
2. Divide students into groups and play waiter and customers at a restaurant.

UNIT 8

你家有几个人

LESSON OBJECTIVES

Language

Students should be able to

- Understand and use the Chinese measure word “个”;
- Employ ritual greetings “认识你很高兴”;
- Understand and use the existential or possessive verb “有”.

Culture

- A brief introduction to China’s One Child Policy

  A typical family in China nowadays has three members: a father, mother and their only child. In order to curb rapid population growth, the Chinese government started the One Child Policy, or Family Plan in the 1970s that permits only one child per family, with some exceptions. For instance, people from minority groups may have two children in one family, and farmers may be allowed to have a second child if the first-born is a girl. If twins or triplets are born in a family, it is considered acceptable in alignment with the policy.

  More related information at: http://www.tcnj.edu/~fisk2/page%204.htm, or http://en.wikipedia.org/wiki/One-child_policy

TARGET VOCABULARY AND SENTENCE STRUCTURE

Vocabulary

人　有　个　认识　高兴

Sentence Structures

(Pronoun/Noun)家有几个人?
(Pronoun/Noun)家有(number)个人.

SUGGESTED ACTIVITIES

Guided Practice

- Bingo

- Fly Swatters

- Listen and Number Workbook
  Ask students to find out what the teacher instructs. The teacher can say "Tom 家有五个人" "心爱家有三个人", students will find the right pictures accordingly.

- Match Workbook
  Draw lines between the Chinese phrases or sentences and their corresponding pictures.

Independent Practice

- The teacher shows a family portrait with many family members. Point to the photo and ask "几个人". After students give the correct answer, the teacher can further ask, "几个哥哥/姐姐". Use as many photos as possible.

- The teacher asks one student "你家有几个人". Prompt him/her to respond by using the sentence structure : "我家有……个人" . Then ask him/her "你有几个哥哥/姐姐". Prompt him/her to answer "我有……个哥哥/姐姐". Ask as many students as possible. As the game goes on, some students can take the lead to ask the questions.

- Get the ball and answer my question.
  The teacher throws a soft ball to some student, whoever gets the ball should answer the teacher's question "你家有几个人" by saying "我家有……个人". If the student gives a correct answer, he/she should be rewarded with a small gift (a sticker or something). When the teacher finds there is no problem with and the students have grasped this sentence pattern, he can move on to another question "你有几个哥哥/姐姐". Later, ask a student to be "the teacher".

- This is my family.
  Students take their family photos and introduce their family to the class by saying: "我家有……个人。这是我的爸爸，这是我的妈妈， 我有 …… 个姐姐和……个哥哥。"

- Pair up your students. Ask them to talk about their own family by looking at their real family photos or the pictures they drew during class time. Their conversations should follow the sentence patterns they learned from this unit:
  - 你家有……个人？
  - 我家有……个人。
  - 你有几个哥哥/姐姐？
  - 我有……个哥哥/姐姐。这是我的……。

- Mini-Play
  Put your students in groups with 5 in each. In each group, one acts as 贝贝 to come to visit Linda's family. Act out the text according to its transcripts. After some time for practicing, each group can act it out for the entire class.

- Family Card Workbook
  The teacher asks students to draw their family members according to each Chinese sentence (我家有……个人、我有……个……). Then write their family members' names. Divide students into several groups and encourage them to share their Chinese family cards with each other. They can keep the Chinese cards in the classroom.

- How Many People in Your Family Workbook
  Count the family members of the four families, complete the sentence under each family picture by filling in the right information, and talk with your neighbors about these families.

- My Family Introduction Workbook

  There are some Chinese characters concerning numbers and family members on the work sheet, together with a passage with some blanks. Fill in the blanks with the information about you and your family in Chinese, and draw some information after the sentences.

- Let's Sing Workbook

♪♫ 你家有几个人 ♪♫

你家，你家有几个人？
我家，我家有五个人。
这是我的爸爸，
那是我的妈妈，
这是我的哥哥，
那是我的姐姐。

ASSESSMENT

Listening

Color the family members according to what you hear from your teacher.

Reading

Match the sentences with proper pictures.

Wǒ jiā yǒu yí ge xiǎogǒu. 1. 我家有一个小狗。	
Wǒ jiā yǒu sān ge rén. 2. 我家有三个人。	
Wǒ jiā yǒu liù ge rén. 3. 我家有六个人。	
Wǒ yǒu yí ge mèimei. 4. 我有一个妹妹。	

A

B

C

D

Speaking

1. Describe the picture.

2. Ask students to work in pairs, asking about the members of each other's families.
3. Introduce your family using your family photo.

UNIT 9

现在几点

LESSON OBJECTIVES

Language

Students will be able to

- Talk about the time and days of the week;
- Ask and answer about the time;
- Ask and answer about weekdays.

Culture

It is important to know the time difference between two locations. Places in different time zones can even be on a different day of the week. The teacher can tell the students about the time difference between China and the city they are in, and talk about the inconvenience in communication or commerce this might bring about.

TARGET VOCABULARY AND SENTENCE STRUCTURE

Vocabulary

中国　美国　现在　今天　点　早上　晚上　月　号　星期

Sentence Structures

现在几点?
今天/昨天/明天星期几?
早上好。
晚上好。

SUGGESTED ACTIVITIES

Guided Practice

- Bingo (for time, week days and dates)

- Fly Swatters (for time, week days and dates)

- Teacher VS Students (for time, week days and dates)

- Listen and Circle Workbook
  Some dates are given on the book. Circle the ones according to what the teacher said.

- Find the Clock
  Give students a paper with some clocks drawn on it. Each clock indicates different time. Ask the students to point to the clock which tells the time the teacher says.

- Draw the Clock
  Students are to draw some clocks showing the time the teacher gives, or the teacher can ask some students to draw on the board. Ask students to tell the time that their clocks tell and see whether they match the teacher's. (Then this becomes an independent practice.)

- Make a Magic Clock
  Give students some cardboards and other tools to make a paper clock with hands that can be moved. Use this magic clock to show different times according to the teacher's instruction "现在……点".

- Find the Day
  Ask the students to take out their class schedule calendar, and find the week. The teacher specifies a week day: prompt students to point to the day on their agenda. This can become a competition for the class. Divide your students into a few groups, each having a calendar to practice with. When they are ready, the competition starts. Ask one student at one time from each group to find the day the teacher calls, the fastest one gets one point for the group. The group who gains the highest score wins and will be rewarded.

The same game can be played to practice dates (……月……号) by using a calendar.

- Design Your Calendar Workbook

Independent Practice

- Play the games ***Find the Clock*** mentioned above in Guided Practice, students, instead of the teacher, take turns to give the time.

- Design Your Clock
  Design your own clock with your own style, draw it on your paper, color it, and indicate the time when the clock is finished. Present it to the class and tell in Chinese what time it was made (the time the clock says).

- Play the game ***Make a magic clock*** mentioned above on Guided Practice, ask student to give the time by saying "现在……点". Or divide students into pairs, one gives a time and the other moves the hands of the clock to make that time. Students can take turns to tell time.

- Students work in pairs and converse about what day and time it is. Present in class and see which pair is the best.
  For example: A: 今天星期几?
  B: 今天星期五。
  A: 现在几点?
  B: 现在10点。
  A: 你去哪儿?
  B: 我去商店。

TEACHING TIP
Make your Chinese class schedule, on which the days of the week should be in Chinese characters. Paste it on students' agendas or on the classroom wall.

- What Time Is It Workbook
  Write the time each clock says.

- Make Your Chinese Calendar
  Each student is given some paper and crayons or markers. Ask them to make a calendar with Chinese features (with both solar and lunar time on it) and mark out the important days on it. Decorate your calendar. Present to the class and tell about the days that are marked out.

- Mixed-up Sentences
  Please look at the instructions (see the Appendix on the back of this book) on how to play this game. The sentences are:
  1.中国现在几点?
  2. 今天是星期三。
  3. 明天是星期四。
  4.中国现在晚上4点。
  5. 美国现在星期几?
  6. 今天是几月几号?
  7. 中国今天五月二十一号。

- Match Workbook
  Draw lines between Chinese sentences and their corresponding pictures.

- Play the Maze Workbook

- Let's Sing Workbook

♪♫ 现在几点 ♪♫

你好，你好，早上好!

今天星期几? 今天星期一。

现在几点? 现在十点。

你好，你好，早上好!

ASSESSMENT

Listening

1. The teacher says a time, students draw clocks.

1.

2.

3.

4.

2. The teacher says weekdays and dates, students mark them out on a calendar.

1.

2.

3.

4.

Reading

1. Draw your clock: give each student an envelope with some notecards specifying various times. Ask them to draw their clocks according to the times on the cards. Glue the cards with the time by each clock.

2. Draw the dates: Give each student an envelope with some notecards of the week days. Ask them to make a weekly class schedule by pasting these weekdays' cards on each day of the schedule.

Speaking

1. Describe the pictures.

2. Students work in pairs, one asks about the time, the other answers, and then they reverse the roles.

3. Students work in pairs, one asks about the weekdays, the other answers, and then they reverse the roles.

UNIT 10

你看你看

LESSON OBJECTIVES

Language

Students should be able to

- Use the adverb “很” plus adjectives to indicate degree, e.g. 很小，很多，很长，很大，很高;
- Understand and use the negation of “是/不是”.

Culture

Students shall understand some issues concerning pets in China. There is a misunderstanding in some western countries that Chinese people treat animals cruelly which is not true. Pets are raised in many families in China and are treated as nicely as they are treated in other countries. Common pets are dogs, cats, fish, birds, rabbits, etc.

Please refer to the following links for more information about keeping pets in China: http://www.bonlive.com/11/60/2030-having-pets-in-beijing-part-1.shtml; http://www.abc.net.au/local/stories/2008/05/02/2233659.htm

About pets health care, please refer to: http://nicelymadeinchina.com/2010/08/21/stone-beck-veterinary-clinic/

TARGET VOCABULARY AND SENTENCE STRUCTURE

Vocabulary

看　鸟　鱼　猫　个子　小　多　长　大　高　很

Sentence Structures

(Pronoun/Noun) 很 Adjective (多/长/大/高)
(Pronoun/Noun) 不是 (Pronoun/Noun)

SUGGESTED ACTIVITIES

Guided Practice

- Bingo
- Fly Swatters
- Teacher VS Students
- Each student picks a flashcard from cards of fish, of bird, of cat and of dog. When the teacher calls a certain animal, the student(s) who has that card stands up and shows his/her card to the class.
- Use body language to act out adjectives. When the teacher says "高/大/小/长", students act them out in one way or another.
- Read and Paste Workbook
  Paste the words of animals on the right animal pictures. (This is to practice reading Chinese characters for the four animals learned in this unit.)
- Listen and Draw
  The teacher says: 小鸟很小 (小猫很大/小鱼很大/头发很长/个子很高/小鸟很多), the students will draw accordingly. The teacher can invite some students to draw on the board.
- Circle the Right Words Workbook
  Circle out the right word of each sentence according to the pictures. (This is a practice of distinguishing "是" from "不是", "在" from "不在".)

- Find My Sister
  Put some pictures of girls on the desk, and ask one volunteer to guess which one is the teacher's sister. When the volunteer selects one picture and shows it to the teacher, if the teacher says "不，那不是我姐姐，我姐姐的头发很长", the volunteer must select another picture until the teacher says "那是我姐姐". Ask more students to participate.

- Find My Brother
  Put some pictures of boys on the desk, and ask one volunteer to guess which one is the teacher's brother. When the volunteer selects one picture and shows it to the teacher, if the teacher says "不，那不是我哥哥，我哥哥的个子很高" , the volunteer must select another picture until the teacher says "是，那是我哥哥". Ask more students to participate.

Independent Practice

- Play the game ***Find My Sister*** and ***Find My Brother***, but ask students, instead of the teacher, to be the one who is looking for his/her sister or brother.

- The teacher shows a toy cat to a student and asks "这是什么". Prompt the student to respond "那是小猫, 小猫很小 (那是大猫，大猫很大)". Then the teacher shows a toy dog and asks the same question to another student. Toy birds, fish and dolls can be employed if variety is desired. As the game continues, ask some students to take the teacher's place to ask the question.

- Put students in pairs; give each group some cards depicting animals (fish, dog, bird, and dog). Repeat the above game. They take turns to ask questions.

- The teacher puts some toy pets outside of the classroom and one student is chosen to go outside to look. When the student comes back, the class asks him/her together "那是什么". That student is supposed to say "那是…….(whatever is put outside by the teacher)，……很小（大）". Encourage as many students to participate as possible.

- This Is Me Workbook
  Divide students into small groups. Give each group paper and crayons or markers. Prompt students to take turns drawing figures with exaggerated body parts and to discuss them with each other. As students are drawing, invite one student at a time to lay on a sheet of large paper on the ground. Trace the student's body with

a crayon or marker. Write the student's name on the sheet and tape it to the wall. Repeat with other students. When all students have been traced, prompt them to stand in front of their sheets and describe themselves. Encourage students to say "这是我，我的眼睛很大，头发很长，个子很高" or "我的眼睛不大，头发不长，个子不高……" Prompt students to exaggerate certain parts of their body and decorate them.

For a simpler way of this activity, see "This Is Me" in Workbook.

- Story Book **Workbook**

- Describe the Card
  Let the students pick one card of animals and ask them to describe the animal on their own card to their neighbors, and then present to the class.

- Mixed-Up Sentences
  Please see the instructions about how to play this game (Appendix on the back of this book). The sentences for this game are:
  1. 你看见了什么?
  2. 我看见了小猫。
  3. 小鸟的羽毛很多。
  4. 小狗的尾巴很长。
  5. 小狗的耳朵很大。
  6. 我哥哥的个子很高。

- Let's Sing **Workbook**

♪♫ 你看你看 ♪♫

你看！你看！小鸟，小鸟。
小鸟很多，小鸟很多。
你看！你看！小鱼，小鱼。
眼睛很大，眼睛很大。
你看！你看！小狗，小狗。
耳朵很长，耳朵很长。
你看！你看！小猫，小猫。
我喜欢呀，我的小猫。

ASSESSMENT

Listening

Under the picture, mark 1st, 2nd, 3rd, and 4th according to what you hear from the teacher.

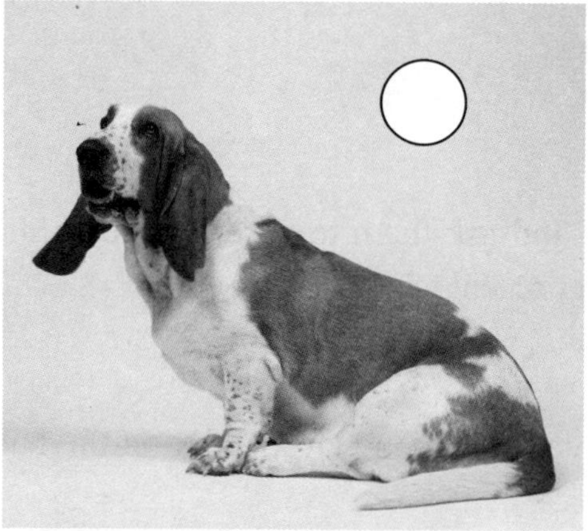

Reading

Match the sentences with proper pictures.

Xiǎoniǎo hěn xiǎo. 1. 小鸟　很 小。		Tā de tóufa hěn cháng. 2. 她的 头发 很 长。	
Xiǎoyú hěn duō. 3. 小鱼 很 多。		Bàba de gèzi hěn gāo. 4. 爸爸 的 个子 很 高。	

A

B

C

D

Speaking

1. Give students a picture book with animals on it. Ask students to describe them.
2. Describe the toy animals (dog, fish, cat and dog) by saying "这是……, ……很……".

UNIT 11

我们去长城

LESSON OBJECTIVES

Language

Students should be able to talk about the location of people and places by using "在".

Culture

The Great Wall of China is a big cultural learning focus in this unit. It is one of the greatest sites and sights in the world. The teacher can introduce the Great Wall starting with its location (North China) by using a map of China, its length is 6260km (about 3890 miles). It is the longest wall in the world. Discuss how it runs, the reasons behind building it (mainly to protect the Chinese Empire from northern invaders), and a brief account of its long history. Also the teacher can play some DVDs on the Great Wall giving students a more direct and vivid picture of it.

Perhaps the most powerful "motto" in modern Chinese history comes from the mouth of Chairman Mao: "Until you reach the Great Wall, you're no hero." (不到长城非好汉.) Figuratively this means "you must overcome difficulties before reaching a goal".

TARGET VOCABULARY AND SENTENCE STRUCTURE

Vocabulary

长城　老师　在　这儿　那儿　见　了

Sentence Structures

(people/place)在哪儿?
(people/place)在 …… (place).

SUGGESTED ACTIVITIES

Guided Practice

- Bingo

- Fly Swatters

TEACHING TIP
There is not much new vocabulary in this unit, so the teacher can use these games to review those words of places learned before: 商店，学校，家etc.

- You are at... (practice for 在)
  In different places of the classroom, put some big flashcards with Chinese characters（长城/学校/商店/Linda家）and pictures of these places on it. Ask one student to find his/her place according to the teacher's instruction. When the teacher says "你在长城", the student is supposed to run to the flashcard with "长城" on it, then the teacher gives another place "你在商店", he will run to the flashcard with "商店" on it. The game continues until the student fails or succeeds in finding all places.

- Where Is the Doggie
  Draw a picture on which there are the Great Wall, a store, a school, a park, and Linda's home. One student volunteer is given a toy dog. The teacher locates the dog by saying "小狗在学校", the student is to move the dog to where the school is. This game can be played with each of students having a piece of this picture paper and a toy dog, or can draw a big picture on the board and one student at a time is to move the dog on the board while the rest will participate too by helping him.

> **TEACHING TIP**
> The teacher can use other nouns students learned before instead of the toy dog, like family members, or even numbers or body parts, to make the game more fun and involving.

- Match 1 Workbook
  Have students draw lines between the sentences and proper pictures.

- Match 2 Workbook
  Have students draw lines between the animals and the places according to what the teacher says.

- Play the Maze Workbook

- Draw the Great Wall Workbook

Independent Practice

- Play the game "You are at..." mentioned above in Guided Practice, but ask a student to give directions. Students take turns to be the director.

- Design a picture with a garden, a school, a store, Linda's home and the Great Wall. Divide students into pairs and give each group a toy dog (or a bird, or a fish), then one student says "小狗（小鸟/小鱼）在长城", the other would move the toy dog (fish or bird) to where the Great Wall is. After the toy dog has "gone" to all places, the students switch their roles.

- Same game tools as the game above, but have one student put the toy dog somewhere first, say in a store, then ask "小狗在哪里". The other student is supposed to answer "小狗在商店". Then the dog is moved to another place, and the conversation goes on. Then, students change their roles.

- Complete the Sentences Workbook

- Hide and Seek
  Set up the classroom like a community near the Great Wall of China. The teacher uses the flashcards in different areas of the classroom to indicate places like the Great Wall, a school, a store, Linda's home. Send out one student volunteer outside of classroom, and let another student hide in one of these places. Then the student who was sent outside comes into the classroom to look for him/her.

While searching, he/she is encouraged to say “ ……(name) 在哪儿”. He has three chances. If he/she finds the hider within these three times, he/she will play the hider, and he/she can have the right to choose the student who will search. When the hider is found out, the entire class (or the student who found him/her) is to say together, “……(the name) 在……”.

- My Day

  Ask students to tell about where he/she is at different times of the day. Give each of them some paper, crayons or markers. They are supposed to draw a clock to indicate the time, write the place to indicate where they are at that time, and themselves in different clothes or with different looks. They can write down the time in Chinese characters (say “8点”) under each clock, and glue words of places under each place. They should color their clocks and places and themselves on the paper. Staple them together into a tiny book entitled **My Day**. Share it with other students by saying: “7点，我在家，8点我在学校……”.

  This project can become **My Father's Day**, or **My Mother's Day**, or **My Sister's Day…**

- Guess Where You Are

  Two students do this game together in front of the class. One chooses a flash card of a place and stick it on the other student's back, and make him/her guess where the flash card says he/she is. The student who chose the card asks: 你在哪儿? The other student responds “我在……” He/she is given three guesses. After 3 times if he/she is not successful, he/she is out of the game. If he guesses correctly, he can be the person who chooses the card, and also gain the right to choose his partner who is going to guess the place.

  Do the same game to practice “去哪儿”.

- Dialogue in Pairs

  A: 我们明天去哪儿?

  B: 去……(a place)。

  A: 明天8点见。

  B: 好，再见。

  After practicing for some time, ask students to perform for the class.

- Survey

  Ask students to make a survey about where their classmates usually go on weekends. Draw a chart on a piece of paper with students' names on the left, "星期六/星期天" on the top of the chart. Talk to all the kids in the class by asking, "星期六/星期天你去哪儿". Students can draw the places if they have difficulties writing Chinese characters for these places. Then present their survey to the class by saying, "……（name）星期六去……, 星期天去……".

- Let's Sing Workbook

♪♫ 春天在哪里 ♪♫

春天在哪里呀，春天在哪里？
春天在我们的眼睛里，
这里有红花呀，这里有绿草。
还有那会唱歌的小黄鹂。
嘀哩哩哩哩哩哩，嘀哩哩哩，
嘀哩哩哩哩哩哩，嘀哩哩哩，
春天在我们的眼睛里，
还有那会唱歌的小黄鹂。

- Let's Chant Workbook

♪♫ 你在哪儿 ♪♫

Linda, Linda，她在哪儿？
Linda, Linda，她在这儿。
贝贝，贝贝，他在哪儿？
贝贝，贝贝，他在那儿。
Tom, Tom, 你在哪儿？
你好，你好，我在学校。
爸爸妈妈在哪儿？
爸爸妈妈在长城。

ASSESSMENT

Listening

The games in Guided Practice (***You are at/Where is the doggie/Match 1/ Match 2***) can be used to assess students' listening comprehension.

Reading

Match the sentences with proper pictures.

Wǒmen qù Chángchéng. 1. 我们 去 长城。		Lǎoshī hǎo. 2. 老师 好。	
Bèibei zài xuéxiào. 3. 贝贝 在 学校。		Māma qù shāngdiàn. 4. 妈妈 去 商店。	

A 

B 

C 

D 

Speaking

1. All the games in Independent Practice can be used as speaking assessment.
2. Divide students into pairs and pretend to call each other over the phone discussing about going somewhere next day and what time to meet.

UNIT 12

“阿不”的故事

LESSON OBJECTIVES

Language

Students will be able to

- Understand how to negate a sentence or a verb or an adjective or an adverb by using “不”, e.g. “不喜欢/不是/不去/不爱吃/不睡觉”. Its intonation is determined by the intonation of its neighboring verb/adjective/adverb. Rules are as follows:
  1. Fourth tone when it is an independent one word sentence or at the end of a sentence or phrase:
     如：不！我不！
  2. Fourth tone except right before a character with a fourth tone, meaning, it is realized as the fourth tone before a first, second or third tone:
     如：不多、不吃 、不喝、不好、不喜欢
  3. Second tone if it is right before a fourth tone:
     如：不去、不看、不爱、不认识
- Ask and answer Yes/No questions.（……吗？）
- Ask about “Who”. (……是谁？)

Culture

In China, to show some certain feelings of closeness, sometimes people call others by putting “阿” in front of the given name of the person when his/her given name has only one character. This is typical in Southern China, not Northern.

TARGET VOCABULARY AND SENTENCE STRUCTURE

Vocabulary

阿　故事　睡觉　电视　澳大利亚　明天　谁　吗

Sentence Structures

不！
不 (verb). (不是，不爱吃，不去，不喜欢，不睡觉)
…… 吗？
…… 是谁？

SUGGESTED ACTIVITIES

Guided Practice

- Where Am I From
  Take to the classroom some small national flags to stand for different countries. Ask one student to pick up the flag of the country according to what the teacher says (我是……人). For example, when the teacher says "我是澳大利亚人", the student must pick up the national flag of Australia.

- Match Workbook
  Ask students to match the person with his/her national flag.

- Ask and Answer Workbook
  Look at the pictures, then answer the questions of "他/她/你是谁".

- Get the Ball and Answer My Question
  The teacher throws a soft ball to a student, who should answer the teacher's question "他/她是谁" while pointing to another student, the student with the ball

should answer “他/她是……(name of that student)”.

- Read and Paste Workbook

- I'm Going to
  Put a pair of flashcards of places in two different areas of the classroom, and ask one student volunteer to follow the teacher's direction. The teacher says “你不去商店，你去学校”, the student must go to the place where the school card is. If he fails, he is out. Use other place cards too for this exercise（商店，Linda/Tom……家，长城……).

- Put a toy dog and a toy bird on the desk, and ask one volunteer student to choose the one that the teacher likes after he/she says “我不喜欢小狗，我喜欢小鸟”, the bird should be chosen. If he/she fails, he/she is out. If he/she is right, he can choose another student to do this game with the teacher. Use other animals or body parts for this game.

- Use the flash cards of food to do a similar game as above. Put the cards (which stand for real food) on a desk, ask a student to pick up the one that the teacher likes when she/he says, “我不爱吃……, 我爱吃……”. If he/she fails, he/she is out; if right, he/she gains the right to choose another student to play this game with the teacher.
  Use drinks（Coke and milk）for this game as an alternative.

- Ask students to take in their family photos (or they can draw one). The teacher would love to know each student's family, so he/she looks at the photos and asks “他/她是谁？” Encourage students to respond by saying 他/她是……. Students may work in pairs and talk to each other about their family members. (Then this becomes an independent practice.)

- Get to Know “贝贝”
  The teacher makes a chart about “贝贝” with information: nationality, the animals he likes and dislikes, the places he goes and does not go after school, the food he likes and does not like, the drink he likes and does not like. The teacher will tell students what “贝贝likes” (where he goes) and dislikes (does not go). Under each item that he likes, the students will mark a smiling face; and under the items he does not like, mark a frowning face. All Chinese characters are marked with Pinyin, also with a picture of each item.

Independent Practice

- All the games above in Guided Practice can be further used as Independent Practice when some student instead of the teacher takes the lead and gives instructions. Make sure students take turns to play the teacher's role.

- Pair your students. Ask them to talk about their own family by looking at their real family photos or the pictures they drew during the class time. Their conversations should follow the sentence patterns:
  1. A: 你家有几个人? B: 我家有……个人。
  2. A: 他/她是谁? B: 他/她是我的……

- Making New Friends
  Divide students into groups with at least 3 students in each. Pretend one student is taking his/her friends to school, and is introducing them to meet his/her classmate(s). Encourage the students who act as the classmate(s) to ask "他/她是谁/那是谁/这是谁". Prompt the student to respond "他/她是……". The conversation can go further by them saying "很高兴认识你（们）". Perform this for the entire class.

- Mr./Ms. NO
  Ask a student to work with the teacher. Whatever the teacher says, he/she always responds "不，我不……" to be a Mr./Ms. NO. For example, after the teacher says "你喜欢小狗吗" Mr./Ms. NO would immediately say "不，我不喜欢小狗，我喜欢小鱼". After the teacher says "明天是周六， 你去商店吗". Mr./Ms. NO responds, "不，我不去商店，我去长城" . After Mr./Ms. NO answers all correctly, he/she can be awarded as the greatest Mr./Ms. NO in history!
  Students can work in pairs for this game too.

- The teacher throws a soft ball to a student, ask him questions like "你是中国人吗". Prompt the student to respond: "不，我不是中国人，我是美国人". All the sentences in the text can be used for this game.

- Students stand in a line, and the teacher starts by asking "你喜欢小狗吗". The student answers, "不，我不喜欢小狗，我喜欢小猫". Then he/she turns around and asks the student behind him/her, "你喜欢小猫吗", then that student will answer negatively too and ask the next student behind him/her. With the game continuing, whoever fails to give a negative answer is out of the game. The last student in the game is the winner and gets rewarded.

TEACHING TIP
Play the same game as above but using food instead of animals. The sentence structure for this game is “我不爱吃……, 我爱吃……”.

- Do a Survey **Workbook**
  Ask students to interview one classmate or a friend about what he/she likes and dislikes about animal, food, drinks, and so on. Present the result to the class.

- Divide students into groups and pretend to be families. They sit together to talk about what to eat for dinner, and where to go on Saturday. Encourage students to disagree with each other by saying, “我不爱吃……, 我爱吃……” and “我不去……, 我去……”.

- Let's Chant **Workbook**

♪♫ 你是美国人吗 ♪♫

贝贝，贝贝，你是美国人吗？
不，不，我不是美国人，我是中国人。
贝贝，贝贝，你喜欢小狗吗？
不，不，我不喜欢小狗，我喜欢小鸟。
Tom, Tom, 你去商店吗？
不，不，我不去商店，我去学校。
Tom，Tom, 我们吃面条。
不，不，我不爱吃面条，我爱吃米饭！
贝贝和 Tom, 去睡觉！
不，不，我们不睡觉，我们看电视。

ASSESSMENT

Listening

The games in Guided Practice can be used to assess students' listening comprehension.

Reading

Match the sentences with proper pictures.

Jiějie bú ài chī shuǐguǒ, tā ài hē niúnǎi. 1. 姐姐 不爱吃 水果，她爱喝 牛奶。	
Gēge bù xǐhuan xiǎomāo, tā xǐhuan xiǎogǒu. 2. 哥哥 不 喜欢 小猫，他 喜欢 小狗。	
Tāmen bú qù Chángchéng, tāmen zài xuéxiào. 3. 他们 不 去 长城， 他们 在 学校。	
Wǒmen bú shì Zhōngguórén, shì Měiguórén. 4. 我们 不 是 中国人， 是 美国人。	

A

B

C

D

Speaking

1. All the games in the Independent Practice can be used for this assessment.
2. Divide students into pairs and pretend to call each other over the phone discussing about going somewhere next day and what time to meet.

Appendix Games

SIMON SAYS

This is a fun game for reviewing vocabulary for guided practice. It is a game for three or more players. One of the players is chosen as Simon (usually the teacher to start with). The others must do what Simon tells them to do when asked with a phrase beginning with "**Simon says**". If Simon says "Simon says jump", the players must jump (players that do not jump are out). However, if Simon says simply "jump", without first saying "**Simon says**", players do not jump; those that do jump are out.

It is Simon's task to try to get everyone out as quickly as possible, and it is every one else's job to stay "in" for as long as possible. The last of Simon's followers to stay in wins.

DOT- TO- DOT

Copy a dot-to-dot puzzle from a children's book. "White out" the numbers and replace them with numbers in a random order. Write the numbers so that the final picture is upside down or side-ways. Provide one student with the puzzle and the partner with a list of numbers in the necessary order to complete the puzzle. As "A" reads the numbers, "B" draws the lines to complete the picture. Students can reverse roles and do a different puzzle. This is especially fun to do just before holidays.

Variation: use the alphabet of picture clues instead of numbers.

FLY SWATTERS

This is a fun game for guided practice, and review new vocabulary.

Preparation

Prepare a visual of the vocabulary pictures.

Game play

- Students are divided into two teams and line up in two lines. The first person in each line (team) has a fly swatter.
- The teacher says one vocabulary item, the person who hits the visual first wins one point for the team.

TEACHER VS STUDENTS

This is a quick and fun way to review vocabulary that focuses on repetition. The teacher says the words over and over again, so students become very familiar with pronunciation and master the vocabulary. This fast-paced game always has the teacher and students laughing.

Preparation

Prepare a visual of the vocabulary pictures.

Game play

- Display the visual and point to a picture. Say a word in Chinese: either the correct word or a "wrong" word.
- If the correct word is said "fangzi" (when pointing at a house, for example), all the students should "chorally" repeat the word.
- If an incorrect word is said "woshi" (when point at a house, for example) the students should remain silent.
- The teacher should point to and say words quickly-mostly giving the correct word, but occasionally making a "mistake".
- If all the students remain silent when the teacher is "wrong", they receive a point. If any student starts to repeat the wrong word, the teacher receives the point. Students love "beating" the teacher.

TEACHING TIP
This game works best when students are just beginning to learn the vocabulary. It's actually a teaching technique! (If the vocabulary is well known, the students always win and it's not challenging or fun.)

HOT POTATO GAME

This quick game with an element of chance is a good way to review vocabulary.

Preparation

- Make flashcards of subjects.
- Get a tennis or other small ball for each team.

Game play

- Divide the class into two, three or four teams and give a ball to the first person on each team. Three rows are optimal.
- When the music starts playing, students on each team pass the ball back and forth until the music stops.
- Then the students holding the balls must stand. Show a flashcard. Whichever of the standing students gives the correct response first wins the point.
- Play continues in the same manner until you use all of your flashcards.

MIXED-UP SENTENCES

This review activity will keep students happily on-task for a long time.

Preparation

- Make up a series of sentences in Chinese that emphasize structures and/or vocabulary that the students are close to mastering.
- Write each sentence in large print on card stock. Cut the sentence apart so that each word is on a separate piece.
- Put all the pieces from a sentence in a zippered plastic bag. Number each bag with a permanent marker.
- Hint: number the back of each word to match the bag number and/or print each sentence on a different color card. This will greatly help you return "lost" pieces to the correct bag.

Directions

- Students may work alone or in pairs at a desk or on the floor.
- Students pick up ONE zippered bag per person or pair. They then move the words around until they form a logical sentence.
- The students write each sentence on their own paper being certain to write the sentence number. If you wish, they may also write the sentence in English.
- Students return the finished sentence pieces in the plastic bag, pick up a new bag and continue the process as time allows.
- Be certain to circulate and give hints to students who may be "stuck".
- As a quick follow-up, call on a student to read sentence 1 (2/3) aloud.

YCT-Friendly Tests

Units 1–6

一、听力

第一部分（第1-5题）

例如：	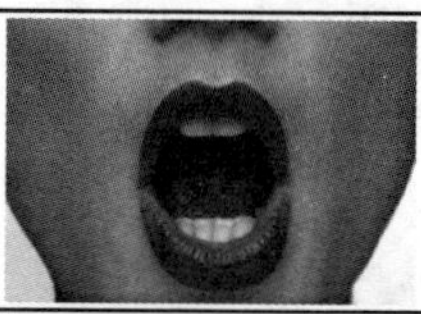	✓
	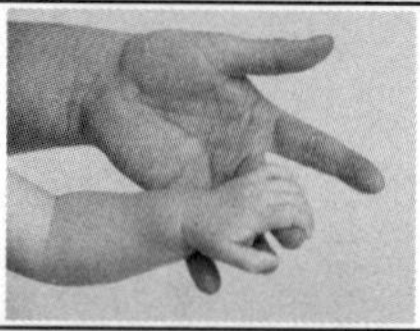	×
1.		
2.	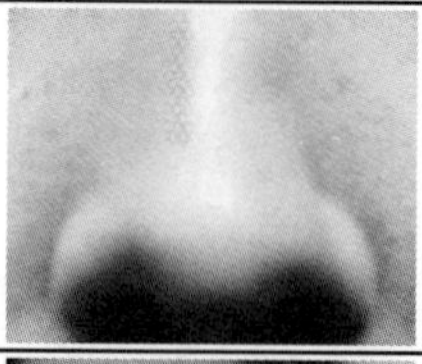	
3.	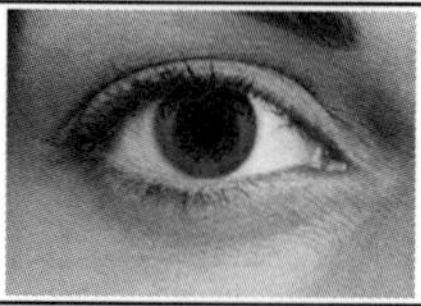	
4.		
5.		

第二部分（第6-10题）

例如：	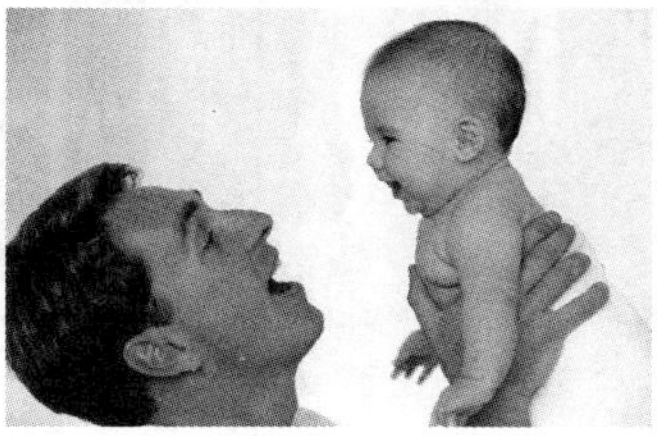 A ✓	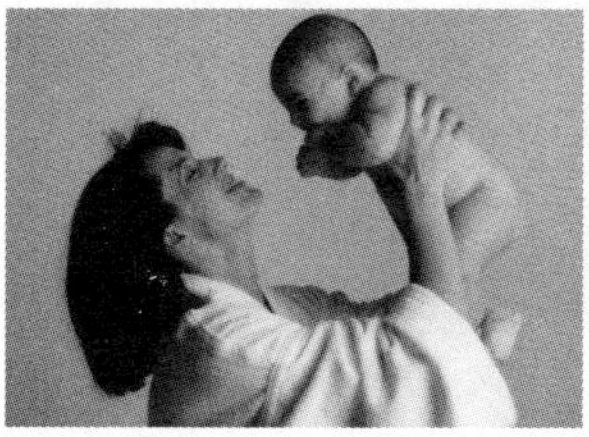 B	 C
6.	 A	 B	 C
7.	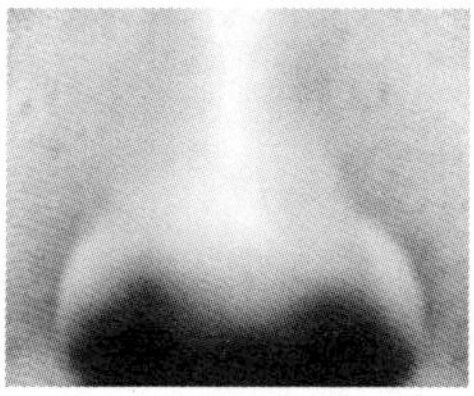 A	 B	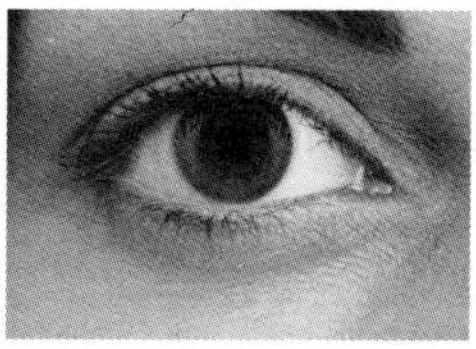 C
8.	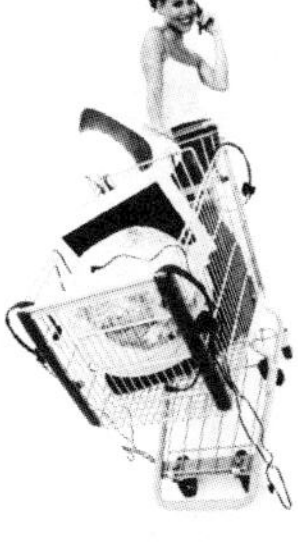 A	 B	 C

9.	 A	 B	 C
10.	 A	 B	 C

第三部分（第11-15题）

例如：		√
		×
11.		
12.		
13.		
14.		
15.		

第四部分（第16-20题）

例如：	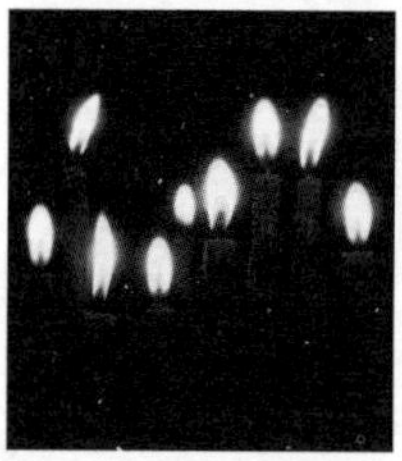 A √	 B	 C
16.	 A	 B	 C
17.	 A	 B	 C
18.	 A	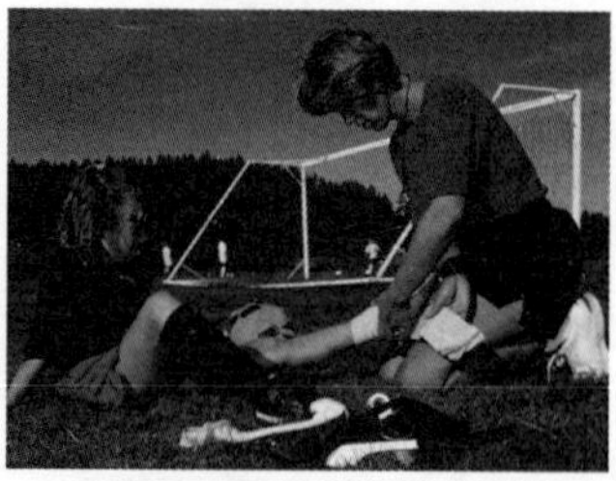 B	 C

19.	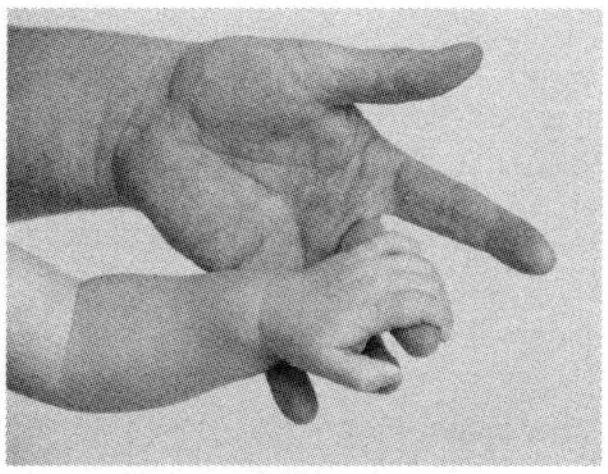 A	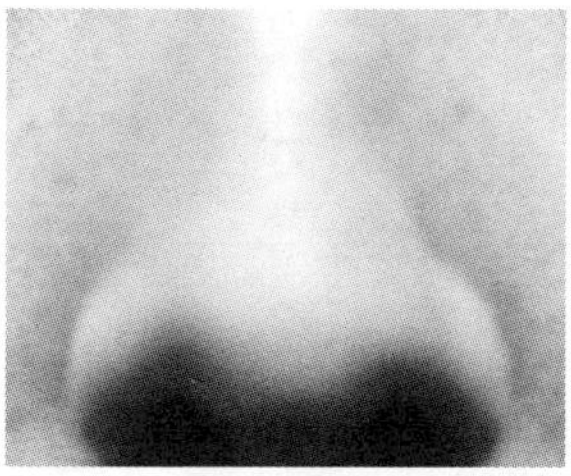 B	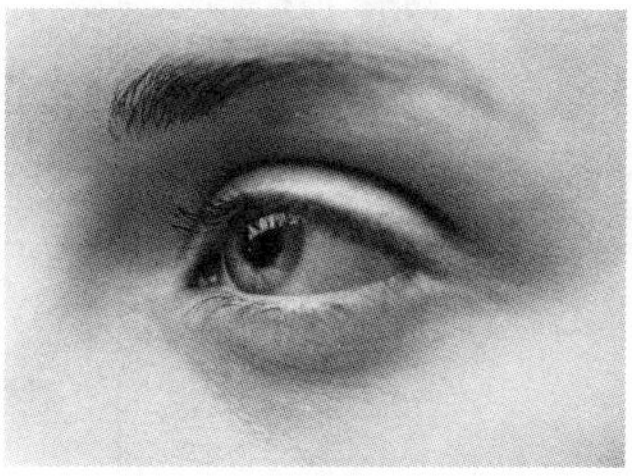 C
20.	 A	 B	 C

二、阅读

第一部分（第21-25题）

例如：	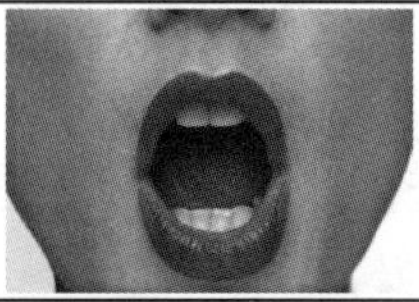	kǒu 口	✓
	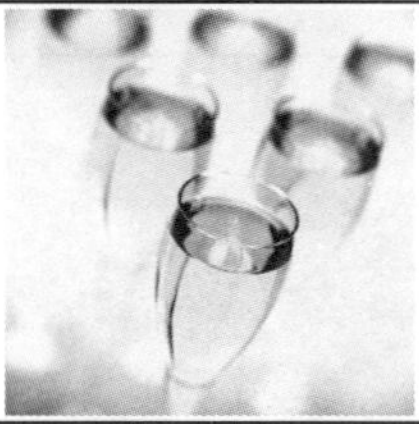	kělè 可乐	×
21.		miàntiáo 面条	
22.		gǒu 狗	
23.		bízi 鼻子	
24.		shāngdiàn 商店	
25.		zàijiàn 再见	

第二部分（第26-30题）

A  B 

C  D 

E  F 

Nà shì shénme?
例如：那 是 什么？ [F]

Wǒ xǐhuan tā de tóufa.
26. 我 喜欢 她 的头发。 [ ]

Zhè shì wǒ de māma.
27. 这 是 我 的 妈妈。 [ ]

Tā qù xuéxiào.
28. 他 去 学校。 [ ]

Jiějie xǐhuan píngguǒ.
29. 姐姐 喜欢 苹果。 [ ]

Shēngrì kuàilè!
30. 生日 快乐！ [ ]

第三部分（第31-35题）

gǒu	hǎo	tóufa	xièxie	shí	shāngdiàn
A 狗	B 好	C 头发	D 谢谢	E 十	F 商店

Nǐ jǐ suì?
例如：A：你几岁？
Wǒ suì.
B：我（E）岁。

Nǐ xǐhuan shénme?
31．A：你 喜欢 什么？
Wǒ xǐhuan tā de
B：我 喜欢 她 的（　）。

Zhè shì shénme?
32．A：这 是 什么？
Zhè shì wǒ de
B：这 是 我 的（　）。

Māma qù nǎr?
33．A：妈妈 去 哪儿？
Tā qù
B：她 去（　）。

Nǐ　Nǐ jiào shénme?
34．A：你（　）！你 叫 什么？
Wǒ jiào Mike.
B：我 叫 Mike。

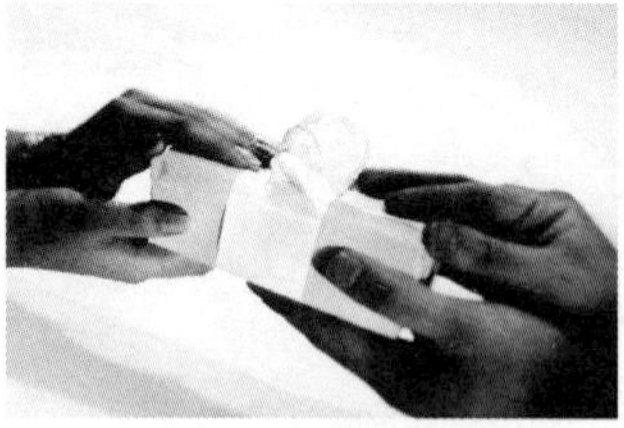

Shēngrì kuàilè!
35．A：生日 快乐！

B：（　）！

Listening Materials

第一部分

（一共5个题，每题听两次。）

例如：口

眼睛

1．头发　2．手　3．眼睛　4．米饭　5．面条

第二部分

（一共5个题，每题听两次。）

例如：我的爸爸

6．我的哥哥　7．她的眼睛　8．去商店　9．生日快乐　10．这是米饭

第三部分

（一共5个题，每题听两次。）

例如：这是他的手。

三个苹果。

11．我五岁。　12．她喜欢小狗。　13．妈妈去商店。

14．这是可乐。　15．我家有四个人。

第四部分

（一共5个题，每题听两次。）

例如：A：你几岁？

B：我九岁。

16．A：姐姐，你去哪儿？

B：我去学校。

17．A：那是什么？

B：那是苹果。

18．A：你好！

B：你好！

19．A：你喜欢什么？

B：我喜欢她的手。

20．A：这是什么？

B：这是米饭。

听力考试现在结束。

（本套试题由本书作者编写。）

Units 1−12

(Official Examination Paper of YCT Level 1)

一、听力

第一部分（第1-5题）

例如：		✓
		×
1.		
2.		
3.		
4.		
5.		

第二部分（第6-10题）

例如：	 A ✓	 B	 C
6.	 A	 B	 C
7.	 A	 B	 C
8.	 A	 B	 C

9.	 A	 B	 C
10.	 A	 B	 C

第三部分（第11-15题）

例如：		√
		×
11.		
12.		
13.		
14.		
15.		

第四部分（第16-20题）

例如：	 A	 B	 C ✓
16.	 A	 B	 C
17.	 A	 B	 C
18.	 A	 B	 C

19.	 A	 B	 C
20.	 A	 B	 C

一、阅读

第一部分（第21-25题）

例如：		gǒu 狗	×
		mǐfàn 米饭	✓
21.		èr 二	
22.	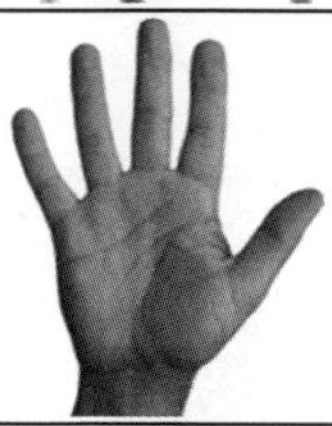	wǔ 五	
23.		sì 四	
24.		bā 八	
25.		qī 七	

第二部分（第26-30题）

A

B

C

D

E

F

Wǒ de bízi cháng.
例如：我 的 鼻子 长。 E

Xiǎomāo, nǐ jǐ suì?
26．小猫， 你几岁？ □

Zhèr yǒu hěn duō niǎo.
27．这儿有 很 多 鸟。 □

Māma ài nǐ, nǐ ài māma ma?
28．妈妈 爱你，你 爱 妈妈 吗？ □

Wǒ xǐhuan hē zhège.
29．我 喜欢 喝 这个。 □

Yǒu rén zài jiā ma?
30．有 人 在 家 吗？ □

第三部分（第31-35题）

xièxie	miàntiáor	rènshi	sān	lǎoshī	xīngqī
A 谢谢	B 面条儿	C 认识	D 三	E 老师	F 星期

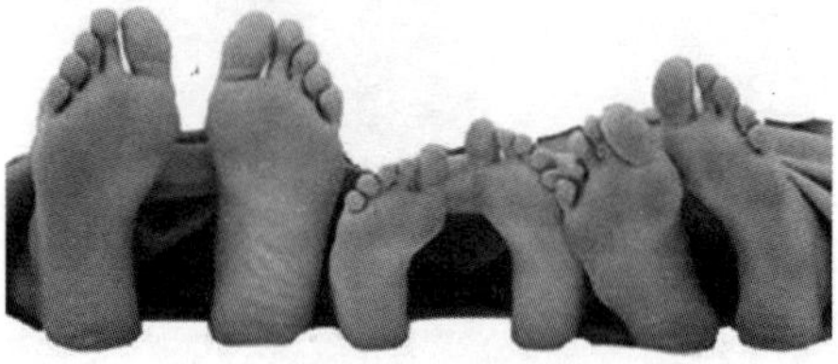

Zhèr yǒu jǐ ge rén?
例如：A：这儿有 几个人？

Zhèr yǒu ge rén.
B：这儿有（D）个 人。

Nǐ hē niúnǎi ma?
31. A：你 喝 牛奶 吗？

B：（ ）！

Nǐ míngtiān qù xuéxiào ma?
32. A：你 明天 去 学校 吗？

Bù, míngtiān liù.
B：不，明天（ ）六。

Nǐ hǎo!
33. A：你 好！

Nǐ hǎo! Hěn gāoxìng nǐ.
B：你 好！很 高兴（ ）你。

Tā shì shéi?
34. A：她 是 谁？

Tā shì wǒ de
B：她 是 我 的（ ）。

Jīntiān chī shénme?
35. A：今天 吃 什么？

Jīntiān wǒmen chī
B：今天 我们 吃（ ）！

Listening Materials

第一部分

一共5个题，每题听两次。

例如：口

耳朵

1．苹果　2．米饭　3．鱼　4．狗　5．哥哥

第二部分

一共5个题，每题听两次。

例如：中国人

6．喝水　7．长头发　8．十四号　9．在学校　10．明天见

第三部分

一共5个题，每题听两次。

例如：我的眼睛大。

现在四点。

11．你的耳朵在这儿。　12．一个大，一个小。　13．我妈妈在哪儿？

14．看我的手，在那儿。　15．我现在去商店。

第四部分

一共5个题，每题听两次。

例如：A：明天是七月几号？

B：明天是七月二号。

16．A：你和爸爸，谁的个子高？B：是我，我高。

17．A：这个月，他去哪儿？B：他去中国。

18．A：你姐姐叫什么？B：她叫爱爱。

19．A：你看，那是谁？B：我不认识。

20．A：妈妈，现在几点？B：现在九点。

听力考试现在结束。

（本套试题为国家汉办考试处提供的YCT一级考试真题。了解考试详情可登录“汉语考试服务网”：www.chinesetesting.cn）

Word List

Pinyin	Character	Unit
A		
ā	阿[4]	12
ài	爱	1
Àodàlìyà	澳大利亚[外]	12
B		
bā	八	3
bàba	爸爸	1
bízi	鼻子	4
bù	不	7
C		
cháng	长	10
Chángchéng	长城[4]	11
chī	吃	7
D		
dà	大	10
de	的	1
diǎn	点	9
diànshì	电视[2]	12
duō	多	10
E		
ěrduo	耳朵	4
èr	二	3
G		
gāo	高	10
gāoxìng	高兴	8
gēge	哥哥	1
gè	个	8
gèzi	个子	10
gǒu	狗	1
H		
hǎo	好	2
hào	号	9
hē	喝	7
hé	和	7
hěn	很	10
J		
jǐ	几	3
jiā	家	1
jiàn	见	11
jiào	叫	2
jiějie	姐姐	1
jīntiān	今天	9
jiǔ	九	3
K		
kàn	看	10
kǒu	口	4
kělè	可乐[外]	6
kuàilè	快乐[3]	3
L		
lǎoshī	老师	11
le	了[2]	11
liù	六	3
M		
māma	妈妈	1
ma	吗	12
māo	猫	10
Měiguó	美国[外]	9
mǐfàn	米饭	6
miàntiáo	面条	6
míngtiān	明天	12
N		
nǎ(nǎr)	哪（哪儿）	5
nà(nàr)	那（那儿）	6
nǐ	你	2
nǐmen	你们	4
niǎo	鸟	10
niúnǎi	牛奶	7
P		
píngguǒ	苹果	6

Pinyin	Character	Unit
Q		
qī	七	3
qù	去	5
R		
rén	人	8
rènshi	认识	8
S		
sān	三	3
shāngdiàn	商店	4
shéi	谁	12
shénme	什么	6
shēngri	生日[3]	3
shí	十	3
shì	是	6
shǒu	手	4
shuǐ	水	7
shuìjiào	睡觉[2]	12
sì	四	3
suì	岁	3
T		
tā	他	4
tā	她	4
tóu	头	4
tóufa	头发	4

Pinyin	Character	Unit
W		
wǎnshang	晚上[2]	9
wǒ	我	2
wǒmen	我们	4
wǔ	五	3
X		
xǐhuan	喜欢	4
xiànzài	现在	9
xiǎo	小	10
xièxie	谢谢	2
xīngqī	星期	9
xuéxiào	学校	4
Y		
yǎnjing	眼睛	4
yī	一	3
yǒu	有	8
yú	鱼	10
yuè	月	9
Z		
zàijiàn	再见	2
zài	在	12
zǎoshang	早上[2]	9
zhè(zhèr)	这（这儿）	6
Zhōngguó	中国	9
Zhōngguórén	中国人	12

注：汉字后括号内的数字“2、3、4”显示该词在YCT大纲中的级别；“外”表示该词为YCT大纲以外的词汇；没有特别标注的词均为YCT一级词。

Introduction to Youth Chinese Test (YCT)

中小学生汉语考试英文为Youth Chinese Test，简称YCT，是一项国际汉语能力标准化考试，考查汉语非第一语言的中小学生在日常生活和学习中运用汉语的能力。YCT分笔试和口试两部分，笔试和口试是相互独立的。笔试包括YCT（一级）、YCT（二级）、YCT（三级）和YCT（四级）；口试包括YCT（初级）和YCT（中级），采用录音形式。

Youth Chinese Test (YCT), a standardized international Chinese proficiency test, is directed at examining non-native primary and secondary school students' ability to apply Chinese language in their studies and daily lives. It consists of two independent parts: a written test and an oral test. The written test is made up of four levels from YCT-Level 1 to YCT-Level 4. The oral test includes YCT-Speaking (Basic) and YCT-Speaking (Intermediate), and the candidates' on-site performance will be recorded.

考试等级 YCT Levels

等级 Level	词汇量 Vocabulary	学习进度参考 Required Preparation (Cumulative Total)
YCT 4	600	按每周2-3课时进度学习汉语二个学期以上 At least two semesters of preparation, at 2-3 study hours per week.
YCT 3	300	按每周2-3课时进度学习汉语二个学期（一学年） Two semesters (one academic year) of preparation, at 2-3 study hours per week.
YCT 2	150	按每周2-3课时进度学习汉语一个学期（半学年） One semester of preparation, at 2-3 study hours per week.
YCT 1	80	按每周2-3课时进度学习汉语3个月 Three months of preparation, at 2-3 study hours per week.
YCT口语中级 YCT-Speaking (Intermediate)	400	按每周2-3课时进度学习汉语两个学期以上 At least two semesters of preparation, at 2-3 study hours per week.
YCT口语初级 YCT-Speaking (Basic)	200	按每周2-3课时进度学习汉语一到二个学期 One to two semesters of preparation, at 2-3 study hours per week.

通过 YCT（一级）的考生可以理解并使用最常用的汉语词语和句子，具备进一步学习汉语的能力。

通过 YCT（二级）的考生可以理解并使用一些非常简单的汉语词语和句子，满足具体的交际需求。

通过 YCT（三级）的考生可以用汉语就熟悉的日常话题进行简单而直接的交流，达到初级汉语优等水平。

通过 YCT（四级）的考生可以运用汉语完成生活、学习中的基本交际任务，在中国旅游时，可应对遇到的大部分交际任务。

a. YCT- Level 1
Examination candidates who reach YCT-Level 1 can understand and put into practice vocabulary and sentences for daily use and have a foundation to pursue advanced Chinese studies.

b. YCT - Level 2
Examination candidates who reach YCT-Level 2 can understand and use simple words and sentences to accomplish specific communication tasks.

c. YCT-Level 3
Examination candidates who reach YCT-Level 3 can use Chinese language to do simple and direct conversations about familiar daily topic, and achieve excellent level in the primary Chinese.

d. YCT-Level 4
Examination candidates who reach YCT-Level 4 can complete basic communicative tasks in daily life and study, and they can handle most communication tasks they encounter when travelling in China.

试卷结构 Test Paper Structure

笔试科目 Written Test	听力题目 Speaking Questions	阅读题目 Reading Questions	书写题目 Writing Questions	时间（分钟） Duration (min)	总分 Total Score	合格线 Passing Score
YCT 1	20	15		35	200	120
YCT 2	20	20		50	200	120
YCT 3	35	25		60	200	120
YCT 4	40	30	10	85	300	180

口试科目 Oral Test	听后重复 Listen And Repeat	听后回答 Listen And Answer	看图说话 Look And Say	回答问题 Speak Your Answer	时间(分钟) Duration (min)	总分 Total Score	合格线 Passing Score
初级 Basic	15	5	5		17	100	60
中级 Intermediate	10		2	2	19	100	60

YCT的目标 The Objectives of YCT

- 激发和鼓励汉语学习热情
- 提高汉语交际能力
- 培养汉语语感和思维能力
- 建立汉语学习的自信心和荣誉感
- Stimulate more enthusiasm about Chinese learning
- Improve Chinese communication
- Cultivate the sense of Chinese and try to think in Chinese
- Build confidence in learning Chinese

成绩报告 Test Score Report

凡参加汉语考试的考生皆可获得对应等级的成绩报告。中小学生汉语考试成绩长期有效。可为检测学校汉语课程的教学效果提供参考。

All examination candidates will receive a test score report of their corresponding level. The test score will be kept valid with a long-term certificate. The score report acts as a reference for primary and secondary schools to evaluate their Chinese programs.

汉语考试夏令营 Summer Camp

为激发海外学生学习汉语的积极性，鼓励其踊跃参加汉语考试，汉办从2008年起设立“汉语考试夏令营”项目。凡在海外参加国家汉办各种汉语考试的考生，皆可以申请“汉语考试夏令营”。具体事宜，考生须咨询考点。

To stimulate overseas students to learn Chinese and encourage them to take Chinese tests, HANBAN launches a project, Chinese Test Summer Camp, starting from 2008 onword. All examination candidates who take the above-mentioned tests abroad are eligible to apply for the Chinese Test Summer Camp. For details, please contact the local test center.

2011年考试时间 Test Dates in 2011

月份Month	日期Date	举办科目Subject
3 月 March	12日（星期六） 12th(Saturday)	笔试 Written Test
5 月 May	14日（星期六） 14th (Saturday)	笔试+口试 Written Test & Oral Test
8月 August	27日（星期六） 27th(Saturday)	笔试 Written Test
11月 November	12日（星期六） 12th(Saturday)	笔试+口试 Written Test & Oral Test

考试日期前一个月在当地考点或汉语考试服务网（www.chinesetesting.cn）报名，考试日期前27天截止报名。详情请咨询当地考点。

Candidates for each examination should register at the test center in their respective countries or at www.chinesetesting.cn one month ahead of schedule. The deadline for registration is 27 days before the test date. Please consult your local Chinese test center for details.

资源分享 Resource Sharing

请登录www.chinesetesting.cn查询更多信息。我们提供大纲和真题集下载、网上报名、成绩报告查询等服务。

报名/成绩查询：kaowu@chinesetesting.cn

综合：kaoshi@hanban.org

Please visit www.chinesetesting.cn for further information. There is both Test Syllabus as well as Official Examiniation Papers in downloadable on the website. Students can register for the test, view scores and perform other inquiries online.

Registration/Grades: kaowu@chinesetesting.cn

General Inquiries: kaoshi@hanban.org

图书在版编目（CIP）数据

阳光汉语教师手册. 1 /（美）刘骏主编. —北京：商务印书馆，2011
（阳光汉语系列教材）
ISBN 978-7-100-08371-3

I. ①阳…II. ①刘… III. ①汉语—对外汉语教学—教学参考资料 IV. ①H195.4

中国版本图书馆CIP数据核字(2011)第092214号

阳光汉语教师手册·1
刘骏〔美〕 主编

商 务 印 书 馆 出 版
（北京王府井大街36号 邮政编码100710）
商 务 印 书 馆 发 行
北京市白帆印务有限公司印刷
ISBN 978-7-100-08371-3

2011年10月第1版 开本787×1092 1/16
2011年10月北京第1次印刷 印张7¼
定价：58.00元